botanical embroidery

30

Effortless Designs That Showcase
the Beauty of Nature

Maggie Schnücker

Creator of Maggie Jo's Studio

PAGE STREET
PUBLISHING CO.

First published in 2021 by
Page Street Publishing Co.
27 Congress Street, Suite 105
Salem, MA 01970
www.pagestreetpublishing.com

Distributed by Macmillan, sales in Canada by The Canadian Manda Group.

25 24 23 22 21   1 2 3 4 5

ISBN-13: 978-1-64567-418-4
ISBN-10: 1-64567-418-5

Library of Congress Control Number: 2021931368

Cover and book design by Rosie Stewart for Page Street Publishing Co.
Photography by Maggie Schnücker

Printed and bound in United States

to nana. Let's get breakfast.

table of

contents

introduction

Hello friend. I'm Maggie of Maggie Jo's Studio. This book of botanical patterns has made quite the journey to reach you now! Whether it's your first time trying embroidery or you're a seasoned lover of the craft, I'm excited for you to stitch these pieces and I'm thankful to you for giving this book a go.

I didn't discover modern embroidery until fairly recently, and I'm very excited you found your way here too. Embroidery is incredibly therapeutic with its rhythmic nature, the sounds of needle and thread pushing through fabric, the feel of the finished stitches. Plus, you get to stab something over and over and it turns into a beautifully textured piece of art.

I started embroidery in 2017 when I was knocked off my feet for health reasons. I'd just graduated college with a degree in graphic design, but I didn't find joy in it like so many people I knew. Nevertheless, I've always loved the intricacies of lettering and of design. One day as I was scrolling through freelance job postings, I saw a finely stitched, hand-lettered embroidery hoop that someone was using as their logo.

I'd never seen anything like it before and I was intrigued. I threw my curls into a scrunchie and flew out the door to my local crafts store. I picked the fabric and a shiny bamboo embroidery hoop, some thread colors, a needle that seemed about right and golden stork snips. Every artist and crafter can relate to the glory that comes with exploring a new corner of a crafts store.

I got home and sketched a million designs full of florals and letters and foliage, and soon I found my niche in colorful botanicals. Two of my greatest loves—greenery and art—had finally met in a way I loved so much.

In just a few months, I'd embroidered myself into a hoop tower. I decided to give selling the pieces a go and started an Instagram and an online shop. My following was growing more and more, and people began asking for patterns of my designs so they could make them too. I didn't even know what that meant, but I thought that maybe all of those hours I'd spent teaching myself the craft could all be gathered in one place so others could learn too.

My patterns started out simply, with a color guide and a drawing. I wasn't sure how exactly to teach people to stitch because I basically made it up as I went along, like a lavish but random pot of soup that made you wish you'd written down the recipe. After quite a bit of reading, constructive advice from patrons and time, I was finally able to write multipage instructional patterns. That led to my monthly pattern subscription, Flourish, which led to this book.

All of that said, I hope you come to this book with fresh eyes. I tend to stray away from classic embroidery techniques and have found my way into the contemporary embroidery world, where freedom and messiness and color in your work are welcome. It's a timeless and wholesome way to create a piece of art, and the experience is fully yours.

Every time you complete an embroidery pattern, it will take on a life of its own in your style. You'll also have your own memories stitched in. When I look at embroidery hoops I've stitched in the past, from as far back as my very first one, I can remember the conversations I was having, audiobooks I was listening to or exact thoughts I had while listening to music. They turn into your own personal little story, whether it's your own design or you're completing a pattern.

I urge you to enjoy the process of embroidery and give yourself grace. Like anything, you'll get better with patience and time. Your stitches will get neater and neater and you'll learn to flow with the thread and manipulate the fibers in a way that creates your vision. No matter what, embroidery will take you to a whole new world of creativity, color and relaxation as you stitch through this book and beyond.

Maggie Schnücker

getting started

As you embark on your embroidery journey, you're going to find many different approaches to the craft. I've illustrated general guidelines for embroidery here, but with time you'll find your own rhythm and ways you like best. I've tried many different fabrics, threads and stitch methods, and this book will take you through my absolute essentials and favorites.

The basic materials needed for these patterns are a 6-inch (15-cm) embroidery hoop of your choosing, a needle, 6-strand embroidery floss, fabric, scissors and a water-soluble marker.

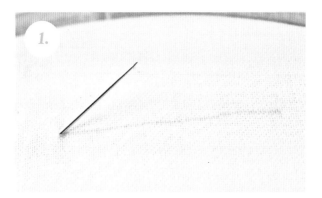

Stitch Guide

Back Stitch

A back stitch is the best way to outline a shape or create stems and branches on your flowers and leaves. Generally, back stitches are all the same length, but I like to allow myself a lot of freedom in length when I'm stitching.

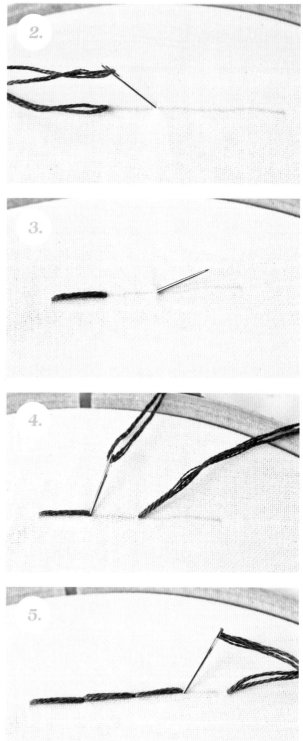

1. Bring your needle up through the fabric from the back of the hoop.

2. Push your needle back down into the fabric about ¼ inch (6 mm) away from your initial hole.

3. Bring your needle up through the fabric again, again about ¼ inch (6 mm) from your last hole.

4. Push your needle back down directly into the previous hole made in Step 2.

5. Repeat as needed.

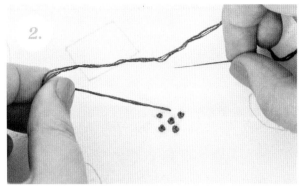

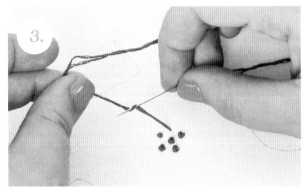

French Knot

French knots are in a love-hate relationship with every embroidery artist I know. I personally love them and think they're a great way to add dimension to a piece. Once you get the hang of them, you'll be using them all the time! You'll need both hands for this stitch, so you might want to practice at a table if you're able. French knots are my favorite way to fill in the center of flowers for that familiar seedy texture, and to fill in other small details like moss and soil.

1. Bring your needle up through the fabric from the back of the hoop.

2. Hold the needle in one hand and pull the excess thread taut with the other hand.

3. Place the needle against the taut thread on the side closest to you. Loop the thread around your needle one, two or three times, depending on how thick you want the knot to be. Remember to keep holding the thread taut.

4. Now, with your thread looped taut around the needle, push it into the fabric directly by your entry hole.

5. As you're pushing the needle into the fabric, hold the thread taut until it creates a knot. Voilà! You did it!

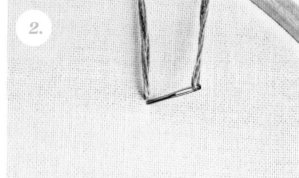

Lazy Daisy Stitch

A lazy daisy stitch is a fun way to add a different texture to your piece.

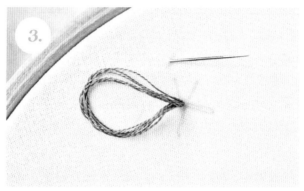

1. Bring your needle up through the fabric from the back of the hoop.

2. Next, push your needle back through the same hole without pulling the thread all the way through.

3. About ½ inch (1.3 cm) away, pull your needle back up through the fabric. Don't pull it tight.

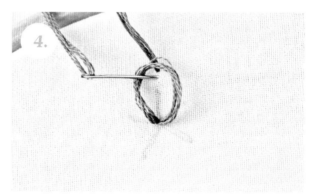

4. Pull your thread enough that you still have a loop remaining. Secure the loop by pulling the thread back down on the other side of the loop.

5. Repeat until you've completed your flower.

Long and Short Stitch

A long and short stitch is the ultimate stitch. It combines a satin stitch (page 14) with a split stitch (page 16) and is particularly great for blending colors. I like using this stitch particularly for bees and flower petals.

1. Bring your needle up through the fabric from the back of the hoop.

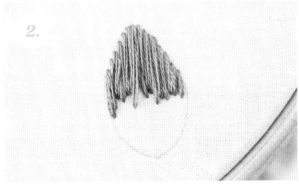

2. Push your needle back down into the fabric. As you make these stitches side by side (just like with a satin stitch), make sure the edge is uneven, meaning some long and some short.

3. Using your next color, continue filling in the shape, but this time push your needle directly into the previous stitches, mimicking the long and short stitches.

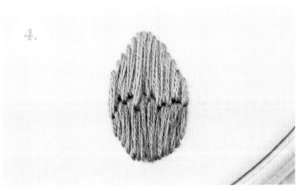

4. Continue until you have filled in your shape.

Satin Stitch

The satin stitch is simply multiple side-by-side stitches you can use to fill in a shape, like leaves and flower petals. There's a lot more versatility than it may seem with this stitch. You can use the same entry spots multiple times and overlap stitches to control the movement. Allow yourself to play around with this stitch to create curves, jagged edges and straight edges.

1. Bring your needle up through the fabric from the back of the hoop.

2. Push your needle back down into the fabric. The length of this stitch depends on the shape you're stitching.

3. Repeat until the shape is filled.

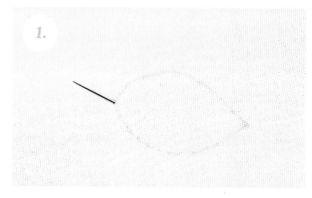

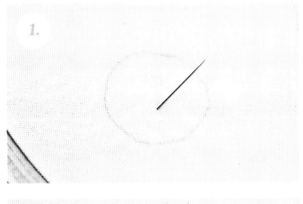

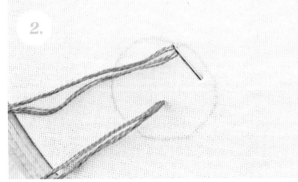

Seed Stitch

Seed stitches are essentially mini random back stitches. In this book, I use them for strawberry seeds (page 59) and prickles on cacti (page 141). They're extra nifty because you can easily replace French knots with them, like in the center of your flowers. If you're not too keen on French knots, simply fill the area with seed stitches to create great texture.

1. Bring your needle up through the fabric from the back of the hoop.

2. Push your needle back down into the fabric about ¼ inch (6 mm) from your initial hole in a relatively random direction.

3. Repeat as needed.

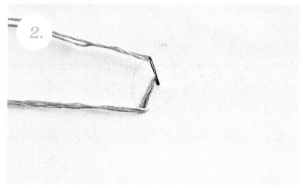

Split Stitch

A split stitch uses nearly an identical method to a back stitch, but instead of sending your needle through the previous hole you will push it directly through the previous stitch. This stitch will help you easily blend colors.

1. Bring your needle up through the fabric from the back of the hoop.

2. Push your needle back down into the fabric about ⅓ inch (8.5 mm) away from your initial hole.

3. Bring your needle up through the fabric again, again about ⅓ inch (8.5 mm) away from your last hole.

4. Push your needle directly into the previous stitch.

5. Repeat as needed.

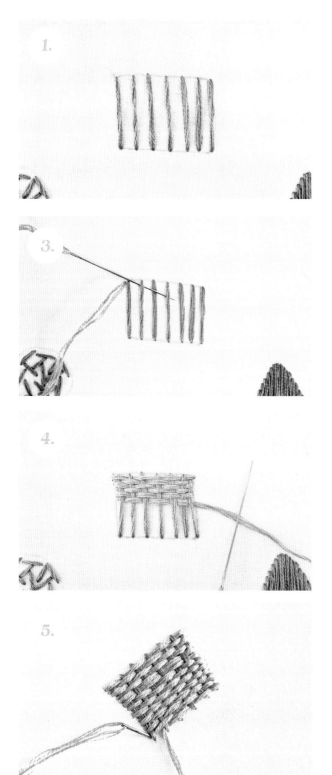

Weave Stitch

A weave stitch is a great way to make basket planters, rugs and blankets in your embroidery piece. It looks complicated, but thankfully it's a simple stitch.

1. Create parallel lines in a row with your thread. Leave space in between each row.

2. Starting from the top, push your needle up through the fabric.

3. Slide your needle under then over each parallel line you made, alternating under or over the thread in a basket-weave pattern.

4. Continue on until you've made it to the bottom of the parallel rows.

5. Push your needle back down into the fabric when you reach the end of the row.

Whipped Back Stitch

I like to call the whipped back stitch the candy cane stitch. While it can be done with one color, I almost always use two. This is the stitch I use when I want to create a twine effect in the floral bouquets of my embroidery piece.

1. Start by laying a base of back stitches.

2. Now, with the same color or a second color, pull your needle up through the first hole of the back stitches.

3. Push the needle under the first back stitch. Then, pass it through on the same side of the next stitch.

4. Repeat this until you reach the end. Then, push your needle back down into the fabric in the last hole of your back stitch foundation.

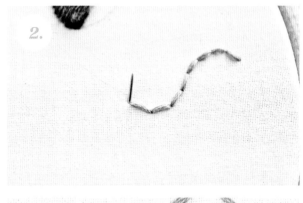

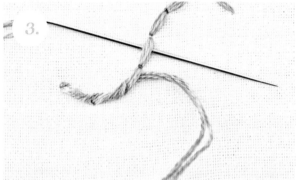

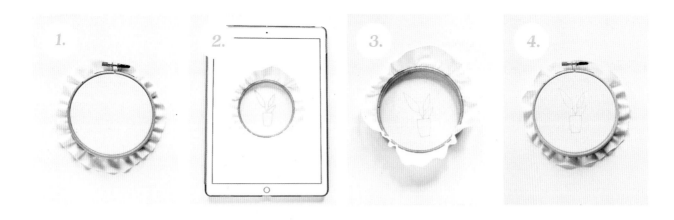

Preparing Your Hoop

When purchasing an embroidery hoop, an investment up front will make the process much more relaxing. If you take anything from this advice, it's to spend the extra couple of dollars buying a nicer, sturdier hoop, rather than settling for a cheaper option. A good embroidery hoop will keep your fabric taut—which is the most important part—and will keep your work looking neat and prevent it from bunching up. I personally prefer wooden hoops, but plastic hoops are just as great.

Choosing fabric is one of the most exciting parts of a project to me, because the color and consistency can completely change the way the finished piece looks. No matter what you choose, I recommend using 100 percent cotton fabric. I really like the Kona® Cotton brand. Pure cotton fabric is perfectly stretchy and firm, which is crucial with embroidery. You need to be able to keep it tight, but it still needs to be stretchy enough to push your needle in and out and stretch evenly inside the hoop.

1. Start by pulling your hoop apart into its two pieces. You'll have an inner ring and an outer ring, the outer ring is the one with the screw bit on top. Place your desired fabric on top of the inner hoop, then push your outer hoop onto the fabric and tighten the screw. From here, you'll pull the excess fabric taut and continue tightening the screw until your fabric is properly stretched.

2. Next, you'll trace your design onto the fabric. This can be done by using your photocopied, printed or cut-out design template placed against a window, lightbox or tablet. Place the hoop facedown so the fabric is flat against the design you will be tracing. In this book, templates have been provided for you at the end of each project for ease of tracing.

3. Using a water-soluble marker, trace the design onto the back of the hoop. Don't stress about mistakes here, as the marker will rinse off when you are finished stitching.

4. Unscrew the embroidery hoop and flip your fabric so the design is now face up. Push the outer hoop back onto the inner hoop and fabric and pull and tighten until it is your desired firmness for stitching.

Dark Fabric

When stitching on darker fabrics, you'll need to trace your pattern on the fabric using a white pencil, as shown above. These markings normally don't rinse off like those of water-soluble makers, so you'll need to be extra careful when tracing.

Threading Your Needle

Embroidery Floss

I recommend DMC® brand embroidery floss and I use the color codes of DMC® throughout this book. I've found it to be less likely to tangle and it's easier to separate the threads to your desired thickness. The brand's thread color selection is also incredible and lends itself to more depth in your projects.

Embroidery thread comes in skeins of floss that are six strands combined. These threads can be easily separated to control the thickness of the area you are stitching. For bigger areas, I tend to use three strands, but for smaller areas like bees (page 57) I'll use one strand. Each pattern will tell you what thickness of thread to use and you can refer to this section at any time to refresh your memory.

Time-saving tip: If you pull the end of the floss from the number side (rather than the logo side), it won't tangle! From there, I recommend using thread bobbins or wooden clothespins to wrap your thread for better storage and to further prevent knots.

Needle

I prefer a size five embroidery needle. The higher the number, the smaller the eye and body of the needle. I've found size five to be exactly right for me and it's my go-to for all of my patterns.

Double Down

When I say I'm using three strands, in reality, I'm using six strands thanks to the thread doubling technique.

1. Pull out and snip about 20 inches (51 cm) of thread.

2. Separate three strands of thread. Using your fingers or a needle threader, maneuver your thread into the eye of the needle.

3. Join the two ends together and tie them in a knot at the bottom. Now you're working with six threads.

This method is my favorite because it keeps your needle from separating from the thread, which lends to a stress-free embroidery experience.

When using 0.5 strands, don't use the thread doubling method. Simply tie a knot on one side of the thread only. This is for ultra-fine details where you're wanting as little thread thickness as possible.

Tying Off Stitches

When you've reached the end of your thread you will need to tie the floss into place. At the back of the hoop, simply create a little knot as close to the fabric as possible and snip the remaining thread. Now you're ready to rethread your needle and continue on.

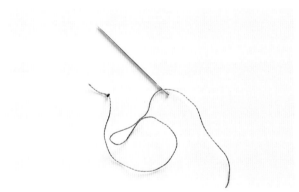

0.5 Strands

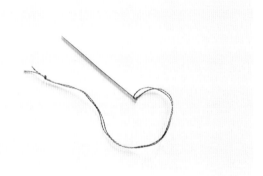

1 Strand

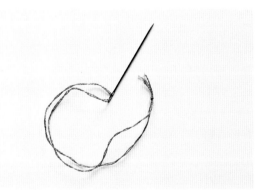

2 Strands

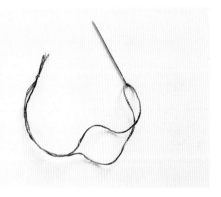

3 Strands

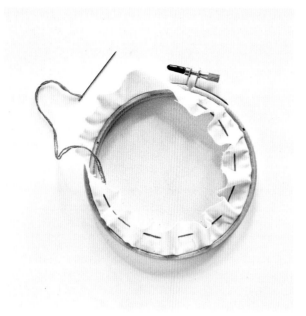

Running Stitch Method

Glue Method

Finishing Your Hoop

Finally, you've finished stitching your pattern. Cut the fabric about 1 inch (2.5 cm) away from the hoop. You can now use a running stitch to tighten the back, or you can use an all-purpose adhesive to glue the fabric down onto the wooden hoop itself. Keep in mind that with the glue method you'll no longer be able to remove the fabric from the hoop should you want to.

I like keeping the back of my embroidery hoops uncovered. I think seeing the colorful network of threads on the back adds to the charm of the piece.

Running Stitch Method

Using the double down method and about 20 inches (51 cm) of thread, you can close up the back of your hoop. Keep 1 inch (2.5 cm) or more of excess fabric, and using an up-and-down stitching motion, follow around the hoop from the top back around.

Glue Method

You can also close your hoop using an all-purpose glue, like tacky glue. Keep 1 inch (2.5 cm) of excess fabric and follow along the wooden ring with a thin line of glue. Press the excess fabric onto the glue and hold it in place.

wondrous wildflowers

No matter where I am, from Texas and Colorado to Spain, I'll always be infatuated with wildflowers. The windows rolled down, a fresh spring breeze and Fleetwood Mac on the stereo while on a wild-flower quest is my dream way to spend the day. I like them on the beach, in a meadow, along the highway and I like them tucked in my sweater pocket. Wildflowers often represent something or someone to people, and I think that's the best thing about them. This chapter is filled with designs of my all-time favorite wild-flowers, and I have a special connection with each of the patterns you'll find here. Thanks to the nature of flowers found in the wild, no two are ever the same or perfect. With that in mind, be free with the flowers you stitch. They'll become uniquely your own as you work with the thread.

Luminous Sunflower

There is a special place in my heart for a lot of things in nature, but no plant seems to grab my attention like the sunflower. They can be three times your height with blooms as big as your face. Every time I see them, I wonder what they are up to. They seem to have personalities given to them straight from the sun and I love that about them. Embroidering sunflowers is my absolute go-to when I'm feeling creatively stuck. They're the ultimate palate cleanser. While you're stitching this sunflower, be sure to experiment with the placement of the different shades of yellow; they can change the brightness and depth of your finished piece.

Materials

Pattern template (found on page 30)

Pen, pencil or water-soluble marker

100% cotton fabric

6-inch (15-cm) embroidery hoop

Size 5 needle

6-strand embroidery floss
(see DMC® Color Guide below)

Fabric scissors and sewing snips

Stitch List

Satin stitch (page 14)

French knot (page 11)

Back stitch (page 10)

356 Garden Rose

355 Carmine

3820 Sunflower Yellow

920 Pumpkin

783 Gold

780 Warm Honey

728 Wild Yellow

830 Brass Olive

754 Soft Peach

898 Pecan

3825 Apricot

3371 Dark Chocolate

367 Soft Emerald

890 Sacramento Green

Luminous Sunflower
(continued)

1. Start by tracing the pattern template with your pen, pencil or water-soluble marker onto the fabric using the Preparing Your Hoop guide (page 19).

2. Begin using satin stitches to create your sunflower leaves using Sacramento green (890). Use 3 strands of floss (page 21) for this step.

3. Using soft emerald (367), begin stitching the remaining leaves with satin stitches. Use 3 strands of floss for this step.

4. Continue using a satin stitch to make the floweret petals using 3 strands of floss. The flowers alternate between apricot (3825), soft peach (754) and garden rose (356).

5. To stitch the middle of the flowerets, use French knots. You can also use seed stitches (page 15) if you choose. Use 2 strands of warm honey (780) for this step.

6. Next, use 1 strand of pecan (898) to make the stems with a back stitch.

7. Using a satin stitch, start making the sunflower petals. I like to start stitching from the middle of the leaf and work my way down each side to create the shape. I start from the smaller petals in the back and work my way to the petals up front. Notice how you can use the hole at the base of the leaf multiple times here too. Where you place the shades of yellow is up to your creative motivations, but I used gold (783) for the petals farthest back, then alternated between sunflower yellow (3820) and wild yellow (728) for the remaining petals. Use 3 strands of floss for this step.

8. When you're finished with the petals, grab your accent colors and, using 1 strand of floss, begin adding in the warm colors to your petals. Alternate between warm honey (780), pumpkin (920), carmine (355) and garden rose (356) as desired. Push your needle up through the back of the fabric into the satin stitches of your petals and then back down into the base of the petals. Repeat on all petals.

9. Begin your French knot center. Create the biggest ring using dark chocolate (3371), the middle ring using brass olive (830) and the center using pecan (898). Use 3 strands of floss for this step.

10. Finally, you're finished with your project and can now close your hoop off using your desired technique (page 22).

Daisy Meadow Cluster

Don't you think daisies are the friendliest flower? They stand as an icon of all things groovy, yet are somehow still the face of delicate beauty. The summer after my husband and I graduated college, we packed his 1999 Jeep Cherokee with camping gear, beach clothes and a white sundress. We drove from Texas to Santa Barbara, California, to elope. We stayed at a beach house bungalow that was adorned with natural floral gardens on the roof. We sat out there and read quite a bit one afternoon and I couldn't keep my eyes off these pristine, white daisies. I knew I wanted to paint them someday. That was before I found embroidery and realized they needed to become a pattern! I hope you enjoy stitching these and feel that California warmth when you look at your finished project.

Materials

Pattern template (found on page 35)

Pen, pencil or water-soluble marker

100% cotton fabric

6-inch (15-cm) embroidery hoop

Size 5 needle

6-strand embroidery floss
(see DMC® Color Guide below)

Fabric scissors and sewing snips

Stitch List

Satin stitch (page 14)

French knot (page 11)

Back stitch (page 10)

3865 White

310 Black

743 Dandelion Yellow

520 Basil

3348 Soft Meadow Green

1. Start by tracing the pattern template with your pen, pencil or water-soluble marker onto the fabric using the Preparing Your Hoop guide (page 19).

2. Begin using satin stitches to create your petals using white (3865). The petals of these daisies are all a little uneven and each is unique, so there's no need to worry about perfection here. Use 3 strands of floss (page 21) for this step.

3. When you're finished with the petals, take black (310) and, using 1 strand of floss, begin adding in the accent details of the daisies. Push your needle up through the back of the fabric into the middle of the daisy satin stitches and then back down into the base of the petal. Repeat on each flower.

4. Now that you're finished with the petals, use dandelion yellow (743) and, using 2 strands of floss and French knots, begin adding stitches in the center of your daisies.

(continued)

Daisy Meadow Cluster
(continued)

5. Next, use 2 strands of the soft meadow green (3348) to make the leaves on the stems using satin stitches.

6. Now, you can finish your project by using back stitches to add the stems with 2 strands of floss. Use basil (520) for this step.

7. Finally, you're finished with your project and can now close your hoop off using your desired technique (page 22).

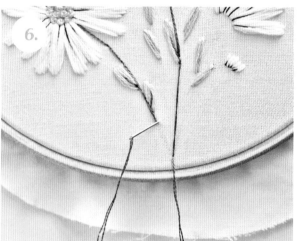

Lush Plumeria Morning

One of my bucket-list must-sees, the plumeria (also known as frangipani) is a super-unique warm-climate flower. I always thought they were interesting, but it wasn't until one of my younger brothers moved to Hawaii to live at a yoga ashram and sent me photos of them in the palm of his hand that I realized just how intricate and incredible they are. This pattern transcends time and space and puts me right on the beach next to my brother. He has a special love for the earth and the pure beauty it puts out, especially when it's tropical. I've seen him belly laugh at a ridiculously big green leaf just because it brought him so much pure joy, which is exactly how this pattern makes me feel. There's so much fun beauty in nature, and I hope you have genuine fun making this pattern.

Materials

Pattern template (found on page 41)

Pen, pencil or water-soluble marker

100% cotton fabric

6-inch (15-cm) embroidery hoop

Size 5 needle

6-strand embroidery floss
(see DMC® Color Guide below)

Fabric scissors and sewing snips

Stitch List

Satin stitch (page 14)

Long and short stitch (page 13)

Back stitch (page 10)

French knot (page 11)

3848 Tropical Teal

895 Pine

972 Mango

922 Navel Orange

3823 Lemon Cream

601 Bright Pink

743 Dandelion Yellow

905 Jungle Green

Lush Plumeria Morning
(continued)

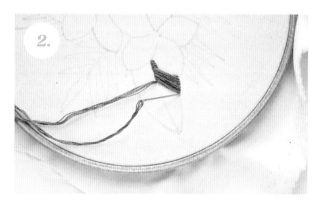

1. Start by tracing the pattern template with your pen, pencil or water-soluble marker onto the fabric using the Preparing Your Hoop guide (page 19).

2. Begin using satin stitches to create your big leaves using jungle green (905). Start from the side of the leaf and push your needle into the center of the leaf. Continue this until you've covered one side of the leaf. Use 3 strands of floss (page 21) for this step.

3. Repeat this on the other side, still using 3 strands of floss, but this time push your needle into the same holes you already created down the center of the leaves.

4. Now, use 2 strands of the navel orange (922) or pine (895) to stitch the body of the palm leaves using satin stitches.

5. Next, use 2 strands of the bright pink (601) or tropical teal (3848) to complete the body of the leaves using long and short stitches. Push the needle directly into the last step's satin stitches.

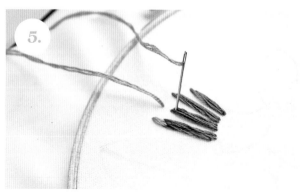

6. Grab bright pink (601) and, using 2 strands of floss, begin adding in the details of the warm-toned palms. Push your needle up through the back of the fabric into the middle of the palm leaves satin stitches and then back down into the base of the leaf. Repeat on each navel orange palm leaf.

7. From here, complete the stems of the bright pink (601) and navel orange (922) palms using 2 strands of floss and back stitches.

8. Now you're ready to start on the plumeria flowers using long and short stitches with 3 strands of floss for the lemon cream (3823) petals. Stitch only about three-fourths of the way down each petal, keeping a jagged edge along the bottom to create a natural look. Do this with the exception of the right side of each flower petal. Take lemon cream (3823) all the way to the middle as pictured; this will create the spinning effect plumeria flowers have.

9. When you're finished, take dandelion yellow (743) and complete the flower with long and short stitches. Continue using 2 strands of floss for this step. Start at the center of the flower and push your needle down through the petal's previous satin stitch until the area is covered. Repeat on all petals.

(continued)

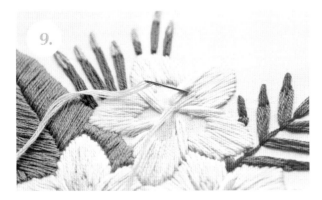

10. Using mango (972), create one long stitch coming from the middle of the flower to just above your center dandelion yellow stitches. This will lay right beside the long lemon cream–colored (3823) long and short stitches you made earlier.

11. Now, top off each flower with a single 3-strand French knot in the center using mango (972).

12. Using pine (895), fill in any spaces between the flowers with French knots to make the piece look more lush.

13. Finally, you're finished with your project and can now close your hoop off using your desired technique (page 22).

Sun-Drenched Blanket Flowers

I'm pretty sure my dad would photosynthesize if he could. This man knows his plants, grasses and flowers. I love being around him all the time, but especially when we are outdoors. Of all the plants I've seen interest him (and most do—he majored in the natural science of range management, after all), blanket flowers are by far his favorites. Raising my siblings and me on our dusty, grassy ranch, he taught us to love the flowers that sprung up suddenly from the dense red dirt. Blanket flowers have very bright melon-colored petals that sharply turn sunflower yellow. They blanket across the sun-drenched land, soaking in the rays and using their bright colors to call in droves of honeybees. If you're like me, a hot pink color like this is a little out of my comfort zone when it comes to embroidery, but that makes these flowers a treat to stitch.

Materials

Pattern template (found on page 46)

Pen, pencil or water-soluble marker

100% cotton fabric

6-inch (15-cm) embroidery hoop

Size 5 needle

6-strand embroidery floss
(see DMC® Color Guide below)

Fabric scissors and sewing snips

Stitch List

Satin stitch (page 14)

Back stitch (page 10)

French knot (page 11)

Long and short stitch (page 13)

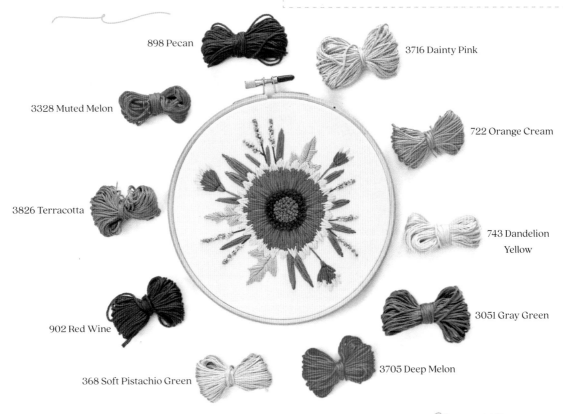

898 Pecan

3716 Dainty Pink

3328 Muted Melon

722 Orange Cream

3826 Terracotta

743 Dandelion Yellow

902 Red Wine

3051 Gray Green

368 Soft Pistachio Green

3705 Deep Melon

Sun-Drenched Blanket Flowers *(continued)*

1. Start by tracing the pattern template with your pen, pencil or water-soluble marker onto the fabric using the Preparing Your Hoop guide (page 19).

2. Using soft pistachio green (368) and satin stitches, begin adding your spiky leaves. Start from one side of the leaf and push your needle into the center of the leaf. Continue this until you have covered one side of the leaf. Repeat this on the other side, but this time push your needle into the same holes you already created down the center of the leaves. Use 3 strands of floss for this step (page 21).

3. Now, use satin stitches to create your dark leaves using gray green (3051). Use 3 strands of floss for this step. I like keeping the edges of the leaf a little jagged for a more natural effect.

4. Using back stitches, make the pecan (898) stems of the pink and orange floral grass. Use 2 strands of floss for this step. You can use this same method of back stitches for the stems of the blanket flowers using gray green (3051).

5. Next, using 3 strands of floss, start making orange cream (722) and dainty pink (3716) French knots. Use an even amount of both colors, but feel free to place the colors along the stem as randomly as you like.

6. Now you're ready to stitch your blanket flower and flowerets. Use 3 strands of floss for the rest of the petals. Using satin stitches, take dandelion yellow (743) and begin stitching the tips of all of the petals.

7. Continue with the last step's instructions, now adding your pinks using long and short stitches. For the petals of the main flower, the bottom layer uses a muted melon (3328) and the top layer uses a deep melon (3705). For the petals of the flowerets, use deep melon (3705).

8. When you're finished with the flowers, grab red wine (902) and, using 1 strand of floss, begin adding in the darker details of the petals. Push your needle up through the back of the fabric into the middle of the flower's long and short stitches and then back down into the base of the flower. Repeat on each flower.

9. For the rest of the pattern, we'll be using French knots to fill the center. The outer ring will use red wine (902) and the center will use terracotta (3826). Remember, you can easily replace French knots with seed stitches (page 15) if you like. Use 3 strands of floss for this step.

10. Finally, you're finished with your project and can now close your hoop off using your desired technique (page 22).

Texas Mountain Laurel

If you've ever been to Central Texas in the very early spring, I'm sure you've seen it lit up with these amethyst-like purple florals. I didn't realize just how gorgeous they were until I met my now father-in-law and saw them through his eyes. A kind and thoughtful man, he holds a dear place in his heart for his people, loose-leaf tea and an intimacy with nature. He's been known to pull the car over and bask in the glory of Texas mountain laurels for a moment and without fail, take a big whiff and say, "Smells just like grape soda!" And they really do! Enjoy all of the curves of the leaves and flowers as you stitch this one and maybe even have some grape soda while you work.

Materials

Pattern template (found on page 51)

Pen, pencil or water-soluble marker

100% cotton fabric

6-inch (15-cm) embroidery hoop

Size 5 needle

6-strand embroidery floss
(see DMC® Color Guide below)

Fabric scissors and sewing snips

Stitch List

Satin stitch (page 14)

Back stitch (page 10)

Long and short stitch (page 13)

17 Mineral Yellow

890 Sacramento Green

986 Cactus Green

153 Lilac

209 Amethyst Purple

29 Violet

1. Start by tracing the pattern template with your pen, pencil or water-soluble marker onto the fabric using the Preparing Your Hoop guide (page 19).

2. Begin using satin stitches to fill in the rounded leaves. Use 3 strands of floss (page 21) in Sacramento green (890) for this step. I like to start stitching from the middle of the leaf and work my way down each side to create the shape. Notice how you can use the hole at the base of the leaf multiple times here too.

3. Continue using satin stitches to embroider your floral buds using amethyst purple (209). On some of the buds, you can see the dark purple heart of the flower. Use violet (29) to fill them in. Use 2 strands of floss for this step.

4. Next, using 1 strand of floss, you can add in the lighter parts of the flowers. Use lilac (153) for this step. Push your needle up through the back of the fabric into the middle of the floweret satin stitches and then back down into the base of the flower. Repeat on flowers with violet (29) showing.

(continued)

Texas Mountain Laurel
(continued)

5. Next, use 1 strand of mineral yellow (17) to outline the Sacramento green leaves with back stitches.

6. Using long and short stitches, start making the cactus green (986) branch. Here, I used 2 strands of floss.

7. Finally, you're finished with your project and can now close your hoop off using your desired technique (page 22).

(page 22).

5.

6.

garden glories

I love feeling the roots of new plants between my fingers, and I love growing things from a seed. I'm certainly not great at it, and I've found that growing a gallery wall of embroidered garden favorites suits me a little better if I really want to see the fruits of my labor come to life. This collection of garden-inspired patterns holds some of my favorite creatures inside, including bees (page 55) and monarchs (page 65). Nothing makes me slow down like embroidery and seeing a monarch float from flower to flower. These pieces will give you an excuse to slow down, smell the rosemary and enjoy a walk through your own personal fiber-art garden.

Forget-Me-Nots, Bees & Rosemary

I can almost hear and smell this summer pattern. Plump bees zooming around florals and rosemary stretching itself across the garden. Inspired by the bees that float around my grandpa's flower and herb garden by the lake, these charming insects and flowerets come together in lots of delicate little stitches. While you're stitching the unforgettable blue of the forget-me-not flowers, don't worry about keeping things neat. Forget-me-nots cluster together and the petals become blurred from a distance. You can think of it like an impressionist painting while you work—the little details will all come together in the end.

Materials

Pattern template (found on page 58)

Pen, pencil or water-soluble marker

100% cotton fabric

6-inch (15-cm) embroidery hoop

Size 5 needle

6-strand embroidery floss
(see DMC® Color Guide below)

Fabric scissors and sewing snips

Stitch List

Satin stitch (page 14)

Back stitch (page 10)

French knot (page 11)

Long and short stitch (page 13)

3052 Sage

830 Brass Olive

310 Black

162 Powder Blue

725 Sunshine Yellow

712 Pearl

783 Gold

3865 White

840 Dried Wheat

937 Lime Rind

Forget-Me-Nots, Bees & Rosemary *(continued)*

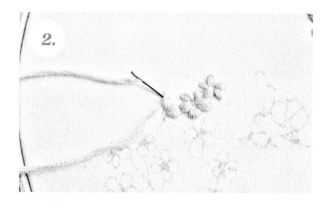

1. Start by tracing the pattern template with your pen, pencil or water-soluble marker onto the fabric using the Preparing Your Hoop guide (page 19).

2. Begin using mini satin stitches to fill in the flowerets of the forget-me-not plant. Use 2 strands (page 21) of powder blue (162) for this step. Each flower is unique, so don't worry too much about each petal being perfectly even with the next. To create a rounded shape for the petals, you can keep bringing the needle down into the fabric at the base of the petal using the same hole multiple times.

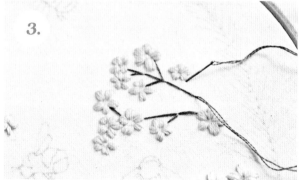

3. When you're finished with the flowerets, grab dried wheat (840) and, using 1 strand of floss, begin adding in the stems of the forget-me-nots. Use a back stitch for this step.

4. Next, use 1 strand of sunshine yellow (725) to make the center of the flowers with French knots.

5. Using medium-length back stitches, start making the rosemary sprigs. Here, I used 2 strands of floss. I alternated between sage (3052) and lime rind (937).

6. When you're finished with the sprigs, use 1 strand of floss to begin adding in the stems. Take sage (3052) and make your stems about halfway down the sprig. Now, use your brass olive (830) to finish the remaining part of the stem of the sprig.

7. For steps 7 and 8, we'll be using long and short stitches to create details in the bees. I used 1 strand of floss for this. Use black (310), sunshine yellow (725) and white (3865) for the body of the bees.

8. Now you're ready to stitch the wings. I used 1 strand of pearl (712) for this step. The top wing should be slightly longer than the bottom wing.

9. When you stitch the legs, use 0.5 strands (page 21) of black (310). Use back stitches for this step.

10. Using gold (783), you can begin adding some darker details to the body of the bees using long and short stitches. Use 0.5 strands of floss (page 21) for this step.

11. Finally, you're finished with your project and can now close your hoop off using your desired technique (page 22).

Floral Strawberry Tart

There's really nothing like a warm, fresh-picked strawberry, or so I've been told. My dad always kept a garden by the side of our house, and it never failed to give us pumpkins, watermelon, okra, cucumbers and butterleaf lettuce. My brother used to grab one of the cucumbers from the garden and eat the entire thing while strolling barefoot around the ranch we grew up on. Sadly, the strawberry plants always seemed to elude us. We'd typically get one single summer strawberry, which my dad would gently wash and cut into the smallest bites for all of us to try. While our lone strawberry was always tart, here's another instance where embroidery gives a low-maintenance alternative. A sweet, embroidered strawberry plant will do just as well!

Materials

Pattern template (found on page 63)

Pen, pencil or water-soluble marker

100% cotton fabric

6-inch (15-cm) embroidery hoop

Size 5 needle

6-strand embroidery floss
(see DMC® Color Guide below)

Fabric scissors and sewing snips

Stitch List

Satin stitch (page 14)

French knot (page 11)

Seed stitch (page 15)

Back stitch (page 10)

3822 Straw Yellow

712 Pearl

3348 Soft Meadow Green

347 Strawberry Red

988 Garden Green

898 Pecan

986 Cactus Green

433 Amber

815 Cabernet

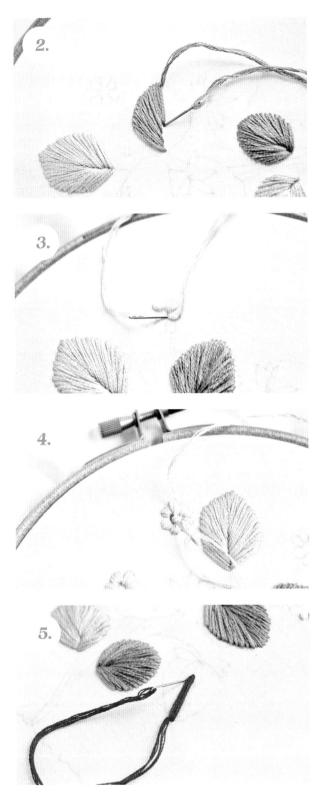

Floral Strawberry Tart (*continued*)

1. Start by tracing the pattern template with your pen, pencil or water-soluble marker onto the fabric using the Preparing Your Hoop guide (page 19).

2. Begin using satin stitches to fill in the leaves of the strawberry plant. Use 3 strands of floss (page 21) for this step. I changed between soft meadow green (3348) and garden green (988) for each leaf, which added some subtle color dimension to the piece. Start from one side of the leaf and push your needle into the center of the leaf. Continue this until you have covered one side of the leaf. Repeat this on the other side, but this time push your needle into the same holes you already created down the center of the leaves.

3. Next, begin on the floral buds. Grab pearl (712) and, using 2 strands of floss, fill in each petal. Use satin stitches for this step.

4. Next, use 2 strands of straw yellow (3822) to fill in the center of each flower using French knots. Remember, you can easily replace this stitch with seed stitches.

5. Using satin stitches, start making the bodies of the strawberries using strawberry red (347). Here, I used 3 strands of floss. I like to start stitching the strawberries from the middle and work my way down each side to create the shape. Take care to leave room for the leaves that will be stitched next.

(continued)

Floral Strawberry
Tart (*continued*)

6. Use seed stitches to make the pearl (712) seeds on the berries. Use 1 strand of floss for this step. Push your needle up through the back of the fabric into the middle of the strawberry satin stitches and then back down a very slight distance away from your entry point. Repeat for each berry.

7. Continue using satin stitches to make the cactus green (986) leaves on top of the strawberries. Here, I used 3 strands of floss.

8. For the rest of the plant, we'll be using back stitches to create the stems. I used 1 strand of floss for this. Back stitches don't have to be the same length, although they generally are. You can make the stems with long back stitches like I did or with mini back stitches if you want more control over the movement of the stems. I used pecan (898).

9. Now you're ready to stitch the soil. Alternate between 3 strands of pecan (898), amber (433) and cabernet (815) to bring some red in to complete the piece. Use French knots for this step. You can also use seed stitches in the soil for added texture.

10. Finally, you're finished with your project and can now close your hoop off using your desired technique (page 22).

Pink Lemonade Coneflowers & Mint

This pattern gives me September vibes! When the last bits of summer on the mint leaves meet with the very early fall monarch migration in Texas, it's my happy place. I remember one fall driving with my grandma in my old truck through the Buffalo Gap area in Texas on an antiquing adventure together. It was very early autumn and we stopped by her lifelong friend's house that had a pasture full of coneflowers right beside it. As we were leaving, a kaleidoscope of monarchs descended on the field of flowers. Somehow with butterflies, there's just as much beauty in one as there is in a whole flutter of them. The details of the wings might look complicated in this pattern, but thankfully they're just two simple stitches and three colors.

Materials

Pattern template (found on page 69)

Pen, pencil or water-soluble marker

100% cotton fabric

6-inch (15-cm) embroidery hoop

Size 5 needle

6-strand embroidery floss
(see DMC® Color Guide below)

Fabric scissors and sewing snips

Stitch List

Satin stitch (page 14)

French knot (page 11)

Back stitch (page 10)

Seed stitch (page 15)

3853 Tangerine

3865 White

3852 Mustard

781 Dark Gold

310 Black

3827 Peaches and Cream

605 Pink Lemonade

989 Spring Green

3350 Fuchsia

895 Pine

367 Soft Emerald

Pink Lemonade Coneflowers & Mint (*continued*)

1. Start by tracing the pattern template with your pen, pencil or water-soluble marker onto the fabric using the Preparing Your Hoop guide (page 19).

2. Begin using satin stitches to fill in the pink lemonade (605) flower petals. Use 3 strands of floss (page 21) for this step. I like to start stitching the petals from the middle and work my way down each side to create the shape. Notice how you can use the hole at the base of the petal multiple times here. Continue with 3 strands of floss and use this same method for the leaves of the coneflower using soft emerald (367).

3. When you're finished with the petals, grab fuchsia (3350) and, using 1 strand of floss, begin adding in the darker details of the petals. Push your needle up through the back of the fabric into the middle of the petal satin stitches and then back down into the base of the petal. Repeat on each petal.

4. Next, use 3 strands of dark gold (781) to make the coneflower center with French knots. Stitch the row closest to the petals. Then, using mustard (3852), fill in the rest of the coneflower. Remember, you can easily switch the French knots to seed stitches if you like.

5. Using satin stitches, start making the mint leaves with pine (895). Here, I used 3 strands of floss. Again, I like to start stitching from the middle of the leaf and work my way down each side to create the shape. Notice how you can use the hole at the base of the leaf multiple times here too. Remember while you're stitching that mint leaves have an irregular edge.

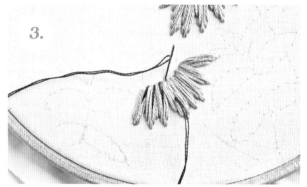

6. When you're finished with the mint leaves, take spring green (989) and, using 1 strand of floss, begin adding in the lighter details of the leaves. Push your needle up through the back of the fabric into the middle of the mint leaf satin stitches and then back down into the base of the leaves. Repeat on each leaf.

7. Next, using back stitches, make the stems. Use 2 strands of floss for this step. Use soft emerald (367) for all of the stems. Back stitches don't have to be the same length, although they generally are.

8. Now you're ready to stitch the monarch butterfly. We'll be using satin stitches to create details in the monarch. I used 2 strands of floss for this. Use peaches and cream (3827) for the lower wing of the butterfly and tangerine (3853) for the upper wing. Notice that peaches and cream (3827) is also used at the tallest part of the upper wing, as is white (3865).

9. Using 2 strands of black (310), fill in the remaining parts of the butterfly, including the body, with satin stitches.

(continued)

Pink Lemonade Coneflowers & Mint (*continued*)

10. When you're ready to stitch the antennae and legs, use 0.5 strands of floss (page 21). Use back stitches for this step.

11. Add more white (3865) details to the monarch using seed stitches over the black (310).

12. Finally, you're finished with your project and can now close your hoop off using your desired technique (page 22).

Rainy Day Perennials

The first time I saw hydrangeas in the wild was one summer when I went to Oxford for a three-week-long watercolor class. As you can imagine, we spent most of our time on nature walks or painting old buildings outside. One afternoon, we'd all spread out around the shady forest area along a meadow to paint and it started pouring rain. I got up from my fallen tree trunk seat to start walking back a different way and I saw real-life sprawling hydrangeas. I've never been so excited to be interrupted during a very focused painting session. I'm introducing a new stitch here, called the lazy daisy, to help give these flowers the color variation and texture they deserve. It'll easily help you blend together the assemblage of petals that make up hydrangea flowers.

Materials

Pattern template (found on page 73)

Pen, pencil or water-soluble marker

100% cotton fabric

6-inch (15-cm) embroidery hoop

Size 5 needle

6-strand embroidery floss
(see DMC® Color Guide below)

Fabric scissors and sewing snips

Stitch List

Satin stitch (page 14)

Back stitch (page 10)

Lazy daisy stitch (page 12)

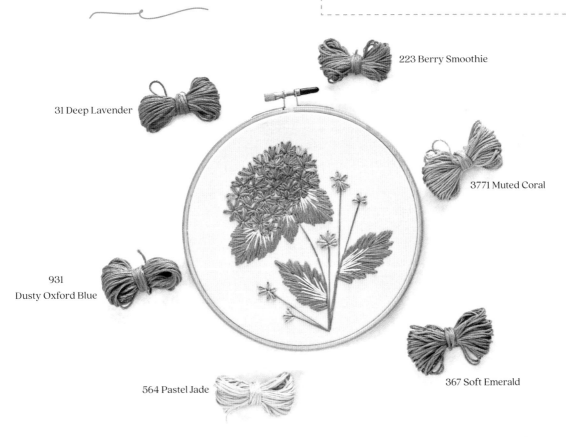

223 Berry Smoothie

31 Deep Lavender

3771 Muted Coral

931
Dusty Oxford Blue

564 Pastel Jade

367 Soft Emerald

Rainy Day Perennials
(continued)

1. Start by tracing the pattern template with your pen, pencil or water-soluble marker onto the fabric using the Preparing Your Hoop guide (page 19).

2. Begin using satin stitches to fill in the leaves of the hydrangea plant. Use 3 strands of floss (page 21) for this step. These particular leaves are rather jagged, so you don't have to worry about perfection as you're stitching. Use soft emerald (367) for this step.

3. When you're finished with the body of the leaves, grab pastel jade (564) and, using 2 strands of floss, begin adding in the lighter details of the leaves. Push your needle up through the back of the fabric into the middle of the leaf satin stitches and then back down into the base of the leaf. Repeat on each leaf.

4. Next, use 2 strands of soft emerald (367) to make the stems with back stitches. You can make them long or keep them short for more control over the shape of the stems.

5. Using lazy daisy stitches, start making the hydrangea petals. Here, I used 3 strands of floss. Stitch the flowerets using muted coral (3771). For the cluster of flowers on the hydrangea, use berry smoothie (223) at the top, deep lavender (31) in the middle and dusty Oxford blue (931) on the bottom. The beauty of clustered florals like hydrangeas is that you can freely overlap the petals and they don't have to be perfectly even.

6. Finally, you're finished with your project and can now close your hoop off using your desired technique (page 22).

2.

3.

4.

5.

Lemon Branch Daydream

My all-time favorite color palette comes to life in this pattern: classic yellow, deep brown and forest greens. This pattern is particularly meditative and relaxing because it's composed of two shapes in three different colors connected with dark brown branches. Thanks to the nature of lemon trees, they don't have to be perfect—each lemon finds its own charming shape to take on as you make this pattern with short satin stitches. Don't be afraid to use the same holes multiple times to help create a curve effect on your mini lemons.

Materials

Pattern template (found on page 77)

Pen, pencil or water-soluble marker

100% cotton fabric

6-inch (15-cm) embroidery hoop

Size 5 needle

6-strand embroidery floss
(see DMC® Color Guide below)

Fabric scissors and sewing snips

Stitch List

Satin stitch (page 14)

Back stitch (page 10)

744 Canary Yellow

3051 Gray Green

838 Walnut

937 Lime Rind

Lemon Branch Daydream
(continued)

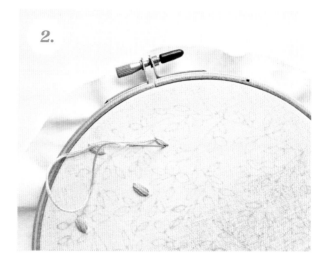

2.

1. Start by tracing the pattern template with your pen, pencil or water-soluble marker onto the fabric using the Preparing Your Hoop guide (page 19).

2. Begin using mini satin stitches to fill in the lemons with canary yellow (744). Use 2 strands of floss (page 21) for this step. Notice how the lemons have a small nodule on the ends. Make the middle stitches slightly longer to create this classic lemon shape.

3.

3. Continue using mini satin stitches to fill in the leaves of the montage. Use 2 strands of floss for this step. I changed between gray green (3051) and lime rind (937) for the leaves, which added some subtle color dimension to the piece. I like to start stitching my leaves from the middle and continue down the sides to create a rounded effect. You can use the same hole at the base of the leaf to help accentuate this.

4. Next, using 1 strand of walnut (838), follow along the branches using back stitches.

5. Finally, you're finished with your project and can now close your hoop off using your desired technique (page 22).

4.

fresh cuts

From irises (page 97) to market tulips (page 103), there's nothing that brightens up a home like fresh-cut flowers. We especially love having them on our breakfast table to make mornings feel new and crisp. These pieces will add a timeless feel to your breakfast nook too! I think the very best thing about fresh flowers is their range of colors. Bright white, apricot or delicate pink, all uniquely glorious. So grab your bouquet of threads, brew some coffee and get ready to stitch an anthology of some of the classics.

Apricot Carnations & Velvety Lamb's Ear

My best friend is a master when it comes to enjoying the little things. She's like a 1950s leading lady with moody overtures playing everywhere she goes. She likes classic, lovely things like fresh carnation flowers and fancy cheeses, but she also likes the unique goodness she finds in the world, like miniature music boxes, banana milkshakes and lamb's ear plants. Pairing timeless apricot carnation flowers with lamb's ear leaves simply had to be done! This sweet bouquet begs to be stitched while popping your favorite classic movie into your old VCR and enjoying a stone fruit tea. It's all about the wild edges when it comes to carnations. The mixture of jagged-edge flower petals and smooth, rounded leaves is what keeps this embroidery piece a refreshing and movement-filled project.

Materials

Pattern template (found on page 84)

Pen, pencil or water-soluble marker

100% cotton fabric

6-inch (15-cm) embroidery hoop

Size 5 needle

6-strand embroidery floss
(see DMC® Color Guide below)

Fabric scissors and sewing snips

Stitch List

Satin stitch (page 14)

Back stitch (page 10)

3341 Warm Apricot

3825 Apricot

3346 Forest Green

353 Coral Ice

3053 Light Sage

3348 Soft Meadow Green

3363 Meadow Green

06 Cloud Gray

Apricot Carnations &
Velvety Lamb's Ear (continued)

1. Start by tracing the pattern template with your pen, pencil or water-soluble marker onto the fabric using the Preparing Your Hoop guide (page 19).

2. Begin using satin stitches to fill in the lamb's ear leaves. Use 3 strands of floss (page 21) for this step. I changed between light sage (3053) and meadow green (3363) for each one, which added some subtle color dimension to the piece. Each leaf is unique, so don't worry about the leaves being exactly the same. Use this same method of satin stitches to add in the little leaves using forest green (3346) along the stems of the carnations. I like to start stitching from the middle of the leaf and work my way down each side to create the shape. Notice how you can use the hole at the base of the leaf multiple times here too.

3. When you're finished with the leaves, grab soft meadow green (3348) and, using 2 strands of floss, begin adding in the stems of the leaves. For the carnation flower stems, use forest green (3346). Use back stitches for this step.

4. Using satin stitches, start making the carnation petals. Here, I used 3 strands of floss. For color variation, I used apricot (3825), warm apricot (3341) and coral ice (353).

2.

3.

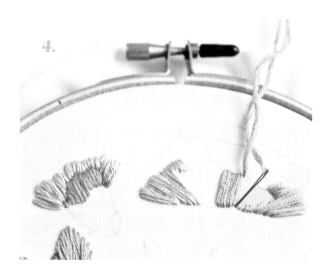

4.

5. For the next part of the pattern, we'll be adding details to the buds and petals. I used 1 strand of coral ice (353) for the accent colors in the carnation petals. Push your needle up through the back of the fabric into the middle of the carnation satin stitches and then back down into the base of the petals. Repeat on each flower petal.

6. Next, use 3 strands of the forest green (3346) to make the base of the carnations with satin stitches.

7. Now you're ready to stitch the vase. Use 2 strands of cloud gray (06) for the little leaves of the vase. Next, using 0.5 strands of floss (page 21), stitch the stems of the leaves. Use 2 strands of floss for the outline of the vase.

8. Finally, you're finished with your project and can now close your hoop off using your desired technique (page 22).

Milk White Crinkled Peonies

My mom is the queen of color. She loves using lots of colors in her paintings and, notoriously, in her home decor. She accents her favorite spaces with tasteful and giant floral arrangements, unique paintings and ranch-style antiques she's collected. She's the only person I've ever met who has managed to mix her love of the blue and white French romantic look with New Mexico eclectic styles—it makes sense if you know her. She's been everywhere and done everything, and she lives to tell the splendid stories and paint the most splendid paintings. Nevertheless, she also knows exactly when simplicity is best, and that's why these peonies make me think of her—she is fanciful and brilliant, like a sunny white flower with perfectly crinkled edges. Peony petals have a mind of their own, so you can enjoy the flow as you stitch them.

Materials

Pattern template (found on page 89)

Pen, pencil or water-soluble marker

100% cotton fabric

6-inch (15-cm) embroidery hoop

Size 5 needle

6-strand embroidery floss
(see DMC® Color Guide below)

Fabric scissors and sewing snips

Stitch List

Satin stitch (page 14)

Back stitch (page 10)

French knot (page 11)

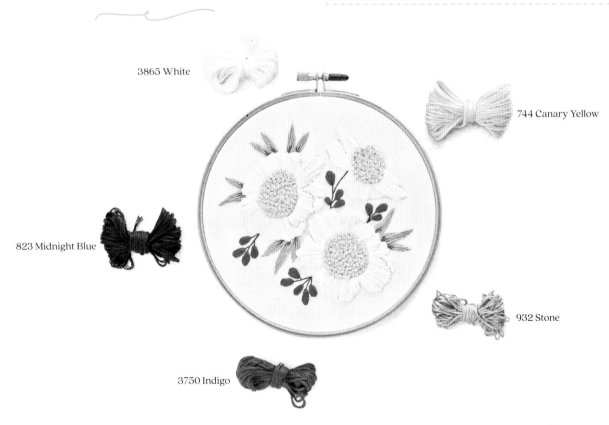

3865 White

744 Canary Yellow

823 Midnight Blue

932 Stone

3750 Indigo

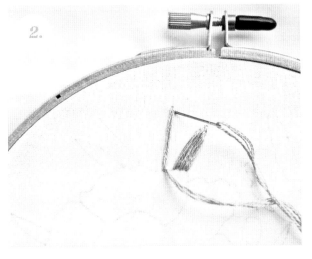

1. Start by tracing the pattern template with your pen, pencil or water-soluble marker onto the fabric using the Preparing Your Hoop guide (page 19).

2. Begin using satin stitches to fill in the stone (932) leaves behind the flowers. Use 3 strands of floss (page 21) for this step. I like to start stitching from the middle of the leaf and work my way down each side to create the shape. Notice how you can use the hole at the base of the leaf multiple times here too.

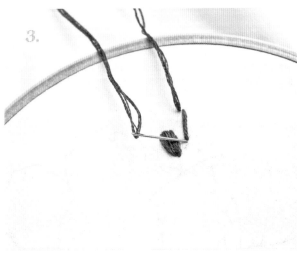

3. Next, use 3 strands of indigo (3750) to make the buds with satin stitches. To create a rounded shape for the buds, you can keep bringing the needle down into the fabric at the base of the bud using the same hole multiple times.

4. When you're finished with the leaves, grab midnight blue (823) and, using 1 strand of floss, begin adding in the darker details of the leaves. Push your needle up through the back of the fabric into the middle of the leaf satin stitches and then back down into the base of the leaves. Repeat on each leaf.

(continued)

Milk White Crinkled Peonies
(continued)

5. Using back stitches, start making the stems of the buds and the tallest peony with midnight blue (823). Here, I used 1 strand of floss.

6. For the next part, we'll be using satin stitches to create the white (3865) petals. I used 3 strands of floss for this. Keep in mind the edges of the peony flowers are uneven, so you don't have to worry about perfection for this bit. Complete the petals farthest back, then the petals on top.

7. Now you're ready to stitch centers. I used 3 strands of canary yellow (744) for the French knots in the middle of each flower. Of course, if you prefer, you can easily swap these stitches out with seed stitches (page 15) for just as lovely a texture.

8. Finally, you're finished with your project and can now close your hoop off using your desired technique (page 22).

Pretty Protea Punch

Protea flowers are on my "dream flowers to see in the wild" list. Native to South Africa and known as sugarbushes, these flowers are sure to draw attention. They also happen to come in many different shapes and colors that look almost prehistoric. This particular protea flowering is known as the firework pincushion protea and is a gorgeous, deep pink. You'll often find them in moody centerpieces and bouquets. I chose to outline this pattern in black thread because I think it really makes the color and uniqueness of its subject pop. I can't think of any other foliage that so perfectly matches its flower's shape. The rounded edges make for a really interesting floral embroidery piece.

Materials

Pattern template (found on page 95)

Pen, pencil or water-soluble marker

100% cotton fabric

6-inch (15-cm) embroidery hoop

Size 5 needle

6-strand embroidery floss
(see DMC® Color Guide below)

Fabric scissors and sewing snips

Stitch List

Satin stitch (page 14)

Long and short stitch (page 13)

Back stitch (page 10)

French knot (page 11)

778 Dusty Rose

3803 Dark Magenta

3687 Punch Pink

505 Jade

223 Berry Smoothie

503 Icy Jade

823 Midnight Blue

310 Black

3750 Indigo

3839 Ice Crystal Blue

Pretty Protea Punch
(continued)

1. Start by tracing the pattern template with your pen, pencil or water-soluble marker onto the fabric using the Preparing Your Hoop guide (page 19).

2. Begin using satin stitches to fill in the petals of the protea plant. Use 3 strands of floss (page 21) for this step. There is a simple gradient to the flower. I started with punch pink (3687), then berry smoothie (223) in the center and dusty rose (778) on top. Each petal is unique in length, so don't worry too much about each petal being perfectly even with the next. When you start the second and third layers, you can use the same holes from the top of the previous layer so your stitches are as close together as possible.

3. When you're finished with the petals, grab dark magenta (3803) and, using 1 strand of floss, begin adding in the darker details of the petals. Push your needle up through the back of the fabric into the middle of the petal satin stitches and then back down into the base of the petal. Repeat on each petal.

4. Next, use 3 strands of indigo (3750) to make the leaves with long and short stitches. Only stitch about halfway up the leaf.

5. Finish the leaves using jade (505). Use long and short stitches to easily blend the green and blue together.

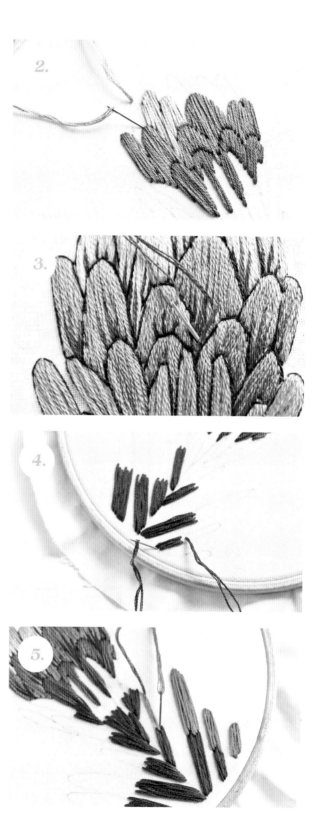

6. Using back stitches, make the indigo (3750) stem. Here, I used 2 strands of floss.

7. Now you're ready to begin your floral buds using French knots. You can easily swap the French knots for seed stitches (page 15) if you choose. For the mini flowerets, use dark magenta (3803). For the bigger floral clusters, use icy crystal blue (3839).

8. For the rounded leaves of these buds, use satin stitches. Use 3 strands of jade (505) for this step.

9. When you're finished with the rounded leaves, grab indigo (3750) and, using 1 strand of floss, begin adding in the darker details of the leaves. Push your needle up through the back of the fabric into the middle of the leaf long and short stitches and then back down into the base of the leaves. Repeat on each leaf. Continue using this color for the stems, using 2 strands of floss and back stitches.

(continued)

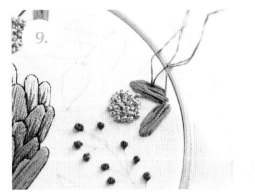

10. Again using satin stitches, you can make the rest of your foliage. Use 3 strands of icy jade (503) for this step.

11. When you're finished with the icy jade leaves, grab midnight blue (823) and, using 1 strand of floss, begin adding in the darker details of the leaves. Push your needle up through the back of the fabric into the middle of the leaf back stitches and then back down into the base of the leaves. Repeat on each leaf. Using 2 strands of floss and back stitches, continue using this color for the stems.

12. Now you're ready to outline your flowers and petals with black (310). Use 0.5 strands of floss (page 21) for this and follow along the edge of each petal, stem and leaf with back stitches.

13. Finally, you're finished with your project and can now close your hoop off using your desired technique (page 22).

Idyllic Irises

My five siblings and I were raised on a ranch in windy West Texas. My grandparents lived a short walk up the road and my grandmother, Iris, always had a stunning and well-kept yard. She kept it bright green and overflowing with honeysuckle. For a very short time every year, her iris flowers would bloom along her fence. Near the end of their bloom time, she'd snip them and put them in jars on her table and on her windowsill. I still think about how excited she would get when they appeared, and now I have one dried and pressed in a frame on my desk. I've dreamt about an iris pattern for a long time, and I'm glad to finally have one for you to stitch now.

Materials

Pattern template (found on page 100)

Pen, pencil or water-soluble marker

100% cotton fabric

6-inch (15-cm) embroidery hoop

Size 5 needle

6-strand embroidery floss
(see DMC® Color Guide below)

Fabric scissors and sewing snips

Stitch List

Long and short stitch (page 13)

Satin stitch (page 14)

French knot (page 11)

Back stitch (page 10)

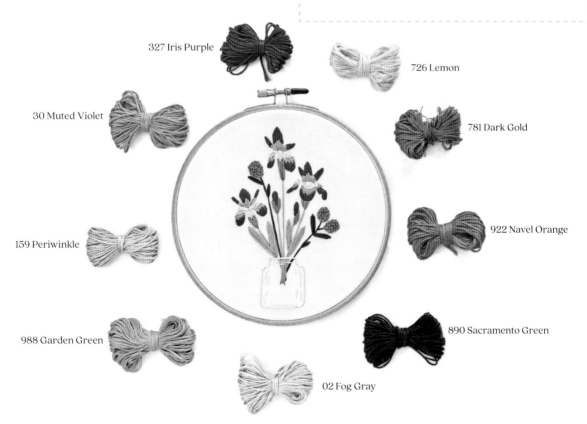

327 Iris Purple

726 Lemon

30 Muted Violet

781 Dark Gold

922 Navel Orange

159 Periwinkle

890 Sacramento Green

988 Garden Green

02 Fog Gray

Idyllic Irises
(continued)

1. Start by tracing the pattern template with your pen, pencil or water-soluble marker onto the fabric using the Preparing Your Hoop guide (page 19).

2. Begin using long and short stitches to make the iris flowers. Use 3 strands of floss (page 21) for this step. Start with iris purple (327) for the edges of each petal.

3. Continue using long and short stitches, now adding muted violet (30), then periwinkle (159). Finally, finish the flower using lemon (726).

4. When you're finished with the top of the flowers, grab dark gold (781) and, using 3 strands of floss, begin adding in the bottom of the flowers. Use satin stitches for this step.

5. Next, use 3 strands of navel orange (922) to make the kumquats with French knots.

6. Using satin stitches, start making the leaves along the stems. Here, I used 3 strands of floss. Use Sacramento green (890) on the kumquat plants and garden green (988) on the iris flowers. I like to start stitching from the middle of the leaf and work my way down each side to create the shape. Notice how you can use the hole at the base of the leaf multiple times here too.

7. For the rest of the pattern, we'll be using back stitches. For this step, make the stems. I used 2 strands of floss for this. Back stitches don't have to be the same length, although they generally are. You can make the stems with long and back stitches like I did or with mini back stitches if you want more control over the movement of the stems. I used Sacramento green (890) and garden green (988) from the leaves for the stems.

8. Now you're ready to stitch the jar. I used 2 strands of fog gray (02) for the outside of the jar and 1 strand of floss for the reflecting details on the inside of the jar. Continue using back stitches for this step.

9. Finally, you're finished with your project and can now close your hoop off using your desired technique (page 22).

Bundled Market Tulips

Picking a color palette for these tulips was so hard because I have such an equal love for all colors of tulips. I fell in love with them on a trip to Amsterdam where they were absolutely everywhere. My grandparents graciously took me on a trip to Europe and we were in Paris for a few days. We decided to take a train one weekend to Amsterdam, and I remember thinking it was kind of comical just how many fields of tulips we saw when riding in. They're very cheery bulbs and it really is a magical experience to see so many of them growing in rows. I decided on light pink because they seem a little less common, and their rarity adds to their beauty. Experiment with different tulip colors if you like! They can easily be swapped around in this pattern.

Materials

Pattern template (found on page 105)

Pen, pencil or water-soluble marker

100% cotton fabric

6-inch (15-cm) embroidery hoop

Size 5 needle

6-strand embroidery floss
(see DMC® Color Guide below)

Fabric scissors and sewing snips

Stitch List

Satin stitch (page 14)

Back stitch (page 10)

Whipped back stitch (page 18)

225 Ice Pink

963 Pastel Pink

522 Hazy Green

3013 Gold Sage

746 Buttermilk Yellow

3862 Soft Walnut

Bundled Market Tulips
(continued)

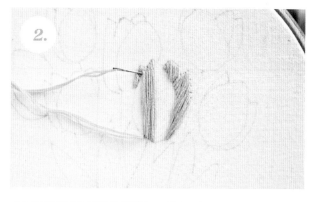

1. Start by tracing the pattern template with your pen, pencil or water-soluble marker onto the fabric using the Preparing Your Hoop guide (page 19).

2. Begin using satin stitches to fill in the tulip flowers. Use 3 strands of floss (page 21) for this step. I changed between ice pink (225) and pastel pink (963) for each flower, which added some subtle dimension to the piece.

3. Next, use satin stitches and 3 strands of floss to fill in the tulip leaves. Use hazy green (522) for this step.

4. Next, use 2 strands of gold sage (3013) to make the stems with back stitches.

5. Using whipped back stitches, start making the twine. Here, I used 2 strands of floss. I used buttermilk yellow (746) as the base color and soft walnut (3862) as the second color.

6. Finally, you're finished with your project and can now close your hoop off using your desired technique (page 22).

forest treasures

Forest treasures are the key to my heart! These patterns are inspired by my love and curiosity for all things foraged, fungi and forest foliage. A favorite adventure of my husband and mine is to road trip to Colorado and explore the mountains and rivers. I always take my journal with me and press my favorite leaves, moss and berries into it, then check on them every few months to see how they look. Getting my hands dirty on a long mountain walk is the best way to spend an afternoon! My hope is that you feel a sense of that natural wandering as you're stitching your way through this chapter. From the slice of walnut tree trunk (page 113) to the juniper sprigs (page 125), you'll feel those freshly foraged vibes with every one of these patterns. Once you've turned on your favorite mountain-trip playlist and curled up with your needle and thread, enjoy your ramble through the forest treasures in this chapter.

Freshly Foraged Lavender

Lavender is a staple in our house, and it's the best smell to unwind with. I don't think my husband was too keen on the smell of lavender when we first got married, but it was nothing a little oversaturation couldn't fix! What could be more relaxing than getting cozy in your favorite embroidery chair to stitch a bundle of lavender? This delicate pattern is all about the simple details. The muted shades of purple and the softness of the stems are sure to slow you down. A lavender bushel wouldn't be complete without adding shades of sage and an elegant ivory finished off with twine.

Materials

Pattern template (found on page 112)

Pen, pencil or water-soluble marker

100% cotton fabric

6-inch (15-cm) embroidery hoop

Size 5 needle

6-strand embroidery floss
(see DMC® Color Guide below)

Fabric scissors and sewing snips

Stitch List

Back stitch (page 10)

Satin stitch (page 14)

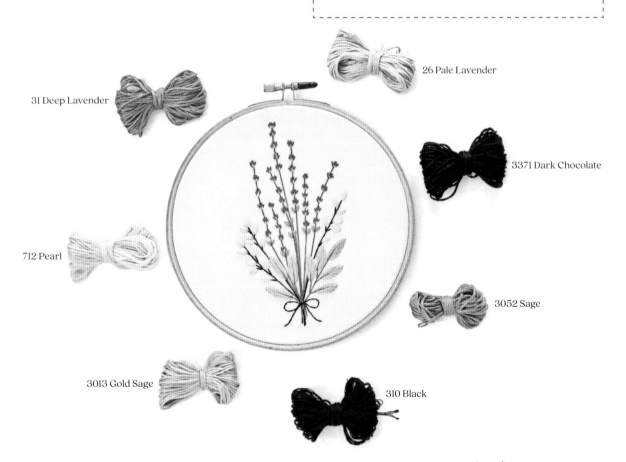

31 Deep Lavender

26 Pale Lavender

3371 Dark Chocolate

712 Pearl

3052 Sage

3013 Gold Sage

310 Black

Freshly Foraged Lavender
(*continued*)

1. Start by tracing the pattern template with your pen, pencil or water-soluble marker onto the fabric using the Preparing Your Hoop guide (page 19).

2. Begin using mini back stitches to fill in the flowerets of the lavender plant. Use 2 strands of floss (page 21) for this step. I used deep lavender (31). Each flower is unique, so don't worry too much about each petal being perfectly even with the next. You can use this same method of mini back stitches to add in the little leaves using sage (3052) at the base of the stems.

3. When you're finished with the flowerets, grab pale lavender (26) and, using 1 strand of floss, begin adding in the lighter details of the flowerets. Push your needle up through the back of the fabric into the middle of the floweret back stitches and then back down into the base of the flower. Repeat on each flower.

4. Next, use 2 strands of pearl (712) to make the buds with satin stitches. To create a rounded shape for the buds, you can keep bringing the needle down into the fabric at the base of the bud using the same hole multiple times.

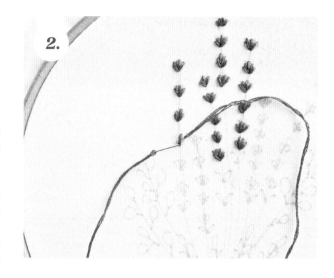

2.

3.

4.

5.

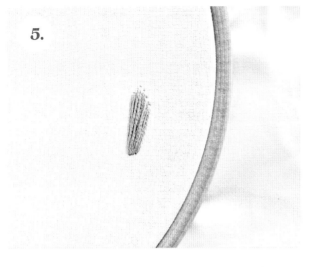

6.

7.

5. Using satin stitches, start making the gold sage (3013) leaves. Here, I used 2 strands of floss. I like to start stitching from the middle of the leaf and work my way down each side to create the shape. Notice how you can use the hole at the base of the leaf multiple times here too.

6. For the rest of the pattern, we'll be using back stitches to create details in the buds and leaves and to make the stems. I used 1 strand of floss for this. Back stitches don't have to be the same length, although they generally are. You can make the stems with long back stitches like I did or with mini back stitches if you want more control over the movement of the stems. I used dark chocolate (3371) for the pearl bud stems and sage (3052) for the lavender stems and for the gold sage stems.

7. Now you're ready to stitch the twine. I used 0.5 strands (page 21) of black (310) for the twine and used very tiny back stitches so I could easily make the black line curves.

8. Finally, you're finished with your project and can now close your hoop off using your desired technique (page 22).

Wild Walnut Wood Slice

True to form for a tree trunk, this pattern filled with satin stitches seems to be one of the pleasantly slower pieces to stitch. I highly recommend sitting outside while working on this one. I found that getting some fresh air and meticulously working on this wood slice made for a very enchanting evening. When you're slowing down with this piece, notice the movement of the satin stitches as you make your way around each ring. The key to smooth satin stitches is to avoid letting your thread get twisted. You can lift up your embroidery hoop and let the needle and thread hang down until the needle stops spinning (kind of like a tire swing), then continue on!

Materials

Pattern template (found on page 117)

Pen, pencil or water-soluble marker

100% cotton fabric

6-inch (15-cm) embroidery hoop

Size 5 needle

6-strand embroidery floss
(see DMC® Color Guide below)

Fabric scissors and sewing snips

Stitch List

Satin stitch (page 14)

Back stitch (page 10)

936 Toad Green

730 Vintage Green

3371 Dark Chocolate

898 Pecan

3828 Caramel

3862 Soft Walnut

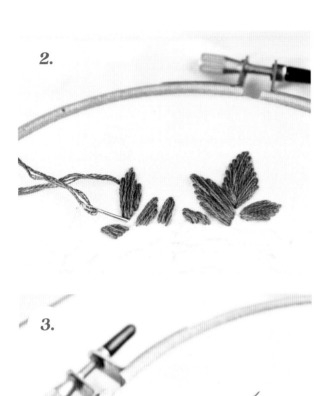

Wild Walnut Wood Slice
(*continued*)

1. Start by tracing the pattern template with your pen, pencil or water-soluble marker onto the fabric using the Preparing Your Hoop guide (page 19).

2. Begin using satin stitches to fill in the leaves around the wood slice with toad green (936). Use 3 strands of floss (page 21) for this step. I like to start stitching from the middle of the leaf and work my way down each side to create the shape. Notice how you can use the hole at the base of the leaf multiple times here too.

3. When you're finished with the leaves, grab vintage green (730) and, using 2 strands of floss, begin adding in the lighter details of the leaves. Push your needle up through the back of the fabric into the middle of the leaf satin stitches and then back down into the base of the flower. Repeat on each leaf.

4. Next, using 2 strands of vintage green (730), use back stitches to add the stems.

(continued)

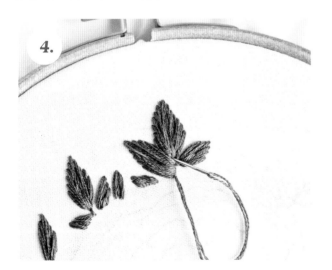

Wild Walnut Wood Slice
(continued)

5. For the rest of the pattern, use satin stitches to start making the bark and inner rings of the wood slice. Here, I used 3 strands of floss. Use dark chocolate (3371) for the outer bark. For the next ring, using pecan (898), push your needle into the same holes from the bark or the last ring; this will keep each layer tight against the previous layer.

6. Continue this until you reach the middle using soft walnut (3862), caramel (3828), soft walnut again (3862), caramel again (3828) and end with pecan (898) for the very center layer.

7. Finally, you're finished with your project and can now close your hoop off using your desired technique (page 22).

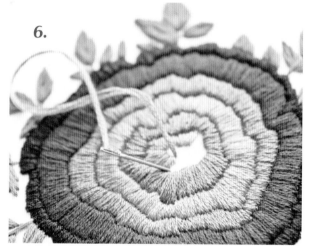

Wild Walnut Wood Slice Template

Night-Blooming Moonflowers

These nocturnal creatures bloom only at night and attract moths, bats and other nightfall critters. The pairing of moonflower and tuberose flower is a classic. Both frosty white, these flowers will add a one-of-a-kind touch to your embroidery hoop collection. These flowers can be stitched on any fabric color, of course, but I chose this muted black to help the little stars and bright whites shine. Also known as tropical white morning glory, this moon-reflecting white flower has a star shape in the center that gives an even more alluring celestial feeling. The petals tend to have a wavy edge, so the more movement you give to the fringe the better.

Materials

Pattern template (found on page 122)

Pen, pencil or water-soluble marker

100% cotton fabric

6-inch (15-cm) embroidery hoop

Size 5 needle

6-strand embroidery floss
(see DMC® Color Guide below)

Fabric scissors and sewing snips

Stitch List

Seed stitch (page 15)

Satin stitch (page 14)

Back stitch (page 10)

Split stitch (page 16)

3865 White

783 Gold

27 London Gray

3047 Champagne

934 Midnight Forest

310 Black

520 Basil

3012 Brass Green

Night-Blooming Moonflowers (*continued*)

1. Start by tracing the pattern template with your pen, pencil or water-soluble marker onto the fabric using the Preparing Your Hoop guide (page 19).

2. Begin using seed stitches to fill in the flowerets of the tuberose flowers. Use 3 strands of floss (page 21) for this step. Each flower is unique, so don't worry too much about each bud being perfectly even with the next. Use London gray (27) for this step.

3. When you're finished with the London gray buds, grab midnight forest (934) and, using 3 strands of floss, begin adding in the rippled leaves of the tuberose with mini satin stitches. You can use this same method of satin stitches for the rest of the leaves. The moonflower leaves use brass green (3012) and the ivies use black (310).

4. Now you're ready to use back stitches to make the stems of your black ivies and tuberose plants. Use 2 strands of floss for this. The tuberose stems are stitched with midnight forest (934) and the ivy stems are stitched with black (310).

5. Next, use 3 strands of basil green (520) to make the vines with split stitches. To create a rounded shape for the swirly vines, make your stitches shorter so you have more control.

6. Using satin stitches, start making the white (3865) moonflower petals. Here, I used 3 strands of floss. I like to start stitching from the middle of the petal and work my way down each side to create the shape. Be sure to leave space for the star shape in the center of your flowers.

7. To stitch the stars in the center of the moonflowers, continue using 3 strands of floss and satin stitches. Use champagne (3047) for this step. Push your needle directly into the previous bright white stitches.

8. For the rest of the pattern, we'll be using back stitches and satin stitches to create the stars, though you can also use French knots (page 11) if you'd like. I used 1 strand of floss for this. Be free with your stitches for the stars; they're reflections of light so they can look as structured or sparkly as you choose. Use gold (783) for this step.

9. Finally, you're finished with your project and can now close your hoop off using your desired technique (page 22).

Crisp Oak & Juniper Wreath

This pattern is inspired by the leaf collections I like pressing into my journal when my husband and I go on road trips. I like gathering the most unique-looking leaves, pressing them between the pages and watching them transform over time. My brother and I like to collect leaves for each other when we go on trips and exchange them. It's funny how pressing botanicals leaves you with preserved stories, just like embroidery. With a natural autumn glow, this color palette is about fresh-pressed forest treasures. Get cozy in your cable-knit sweater, put on a record and relish in the warm auburns, antique oranges and winter berry blues.

Materials

Pattern template (found on page 128)

Pen, pencil or water-soluble marker

100% cotton fabric

6-inch (15-cm) embroidery hoop

Size 5 needle

6-strand embroidery floss
(see DMC® Color Guide below)

Fabric scissors and sewing snips

Stitch List

Seed stitch (page 15)

Satin stitch (page 14)

Back stitch (page 10)

3862 Soft Walnut

437 Desert Sand

221 Deep Currant

830 Brass Olive

300 Toasted Chestnut

930 Winter Berry Blue

780 Warm Honey

561 Juniper

Crisp Oak & Juniper Wreath (*continued*)

1. Start by tracing the pattern template with your pen, pencil or water-soluble marker onto the fabric using the Preparing Your Hoop guide (page 19).

2. Begin using seed stitches to make the sprigs of the juniper (561) branch. Use 2 strands of floss (page 21) for this step.

3. Grab winter berry blue (930) and, using satin stitches, make the berries on the branches. I used 2 strands of floss for this step.

4. Now you can add your branches using soft walnut (3862). Use 1 strand of floss to back stitch your branches.

5. Using satin stitches, make the body of your acorn using desert sand (437). Use 3 strands of floss for this step.

6. You can now add the hats on top of the acorns using seed stitches. Grab soft walnut (3862) for this step and use 1 strand of floss.

7. Next, use satin stitches to make your oak leaves. I alternated between toasted chestnut (300), warm honey (780) and deep currant (221) for this step. Start from one side of the leaf and push your needle into the center of the leaf. Continue this until you have covered one side of the leaf. Repeat this on the other side, but this time push your needle into the same holes you already created down the center of the leaves.

8. Now you're ready to add the details to your leaves using brass olive (830) and 1 strand of floss. Push your needle up through the back of the fabric into the middle of the leaf satin stitches and then back down into the base of the leaf. Repeat on each leaf.

9. Next, use 2 strands of brass olive (830) to make the stems of the oak leaves with back stitches.

10. Finally, you're finished with your project and can now close your hoop off using your desired technique (page 22).

Moss Patch & Ruby Toadstools

Is there someone in your life who just seems to completely become themselves in the forest? My husband is my favorite window into woodlands. He's a metaphysically curious, nature-loving creature with a special interest in fungi. Nothing seems to invigorate him more than cool shady forest breezes, lace-up boots and seeing a mushroom in the wild. Sometimes I wonder how he is so surprised every time we see them, as if maybe he doubts they are real and then sees one and fully believes its magic. There is a childlike joy in venturing into the forest, and that's the vibe I get when stitching this pattern. There are a lot of French knots here (or seed stitches, if you prefer), but when you finish, they come together with a natural mossy texture that is well worth it!

Materials

Pattern template (found on page 133)

Pen, pencil or water-soluble marker

100% cotton fabric

6-inch (15-cm) embroidery hoop

Size 5 needle

6-strand embroidery floss
(see DMC® Color Guide below)

Fabric scissors and sewing snips

Stitch List

Satin stitch (page 14)

Back stitch (page 10)

French knot (page 11)

Long and short stitch (page 13)

3052 Sage

938 Coffee Brown

739 Ivory

3051 Gray Green

738 Cream

319 Dark Emerald

3777 Ruby Red

470 Bright Lime

580 Avocado Green

3346 Forest Green

472 Chartreuse

371 Granola

Moss Patch & Ruby Toadstools (*continued*)

1. Start by tracing the pattern template with your pen, pencil or water-soluble marker onto the fabric using the Preparing Your Hoop guide (page 19).

2. Use satin stitches to fill in the rippled ferns. Use 3 strands of floss (page 21) for this step. I changed between gray green (3051) and sage (3052) for each fern, which added some subtle color dimension to the piece.

3. When you're finished with the fern leaves, grab coffee brown (938) and, using 1 strand of floss, begin adding in the stems of the ferns. Use back stitches for this step.

4. Next, use 3 strands of ivory (739) to make the bottoms of the middle and farthest right mushrooms about a quarter of the way down. For the rest of the base and for the smallest mushroom on the left, use cream (738). This adds a little bit of color dimension. Use satin stitches for this step.

5. Continue using satin stitches to make the mushroom caps with ruby red (3777). Here, I used 2 strands of floss. Make the stitches longer near the bottom and shorter as you go up for a rounded effect.

(continued)

Moss Patch & Ruby Toadstools (*continued*)

6. Using French knots, or seed stitches (page 15) if you prefer, make the speckles of the toadstool caps. Use 1 strand of ivory (739) for this step.

7. Now you're ready to begin making your moss. I used 2 strands of floss for this. Don't forget, you can easily use seed stitches if you prefer, but I used French knots for this step. Notice how some of the moss is within the circle and some is drooping over the edge. For the left side's moss, fill in most of the area with avocado green (580). Then, fill in the remaining spaces with chartreuse (472) and granola (371). For the right side's moss, fill in most of the area with dark emerald (319). Then, fill in the remaining spaces with forest green (3346) and bright lime (470).

8. Using coffee brown (938), you can begin outlining and adding some darker details to the body of the mushrooms using long and short stitches. Use 0.5 strands of floss (page 21) for this step.

9. Now you're ready to stitch the circular border. I used 1 strand of coffee brown (938) for this. Follow along the line using back stitches.

10. Finally, you're finished with your project and can now close your hoop off using your desired technique (page 22).

Moss Patch & Ruby Toadstools Template

desert finds

This collection of hoops is going to take you on a desert journey, minus the heat and rattlesnakes, from my favorite deserts in California and Arizona, to my desert home in Texas. Cacti, red dirt and desert foliage are particularly nostalgic for me growing up in West Texas. No matter how much I like to think the best places on earth are rainy, I always end up with a rooted and homey feeling when I'm around plants growing out of cracked earth. True to form, one of the reasons I fell in love with embroidery was because of a neatly stitched cactus I saw in a cabana coffee shop in California. You'll needle and thread your way through multiple types of cacti and desert scenes as you move through this chapter, though I hope you find yourself in a cool, air-conditioned space while you do so.

Warm Desert Mirage

In this pattern, we have a mirage of one of my very favorite places that my husband and I have camped: Saguaro National Park. We camped there for two nights one summer, as part of a larger road trip. The first night, we were thoroughly unprepared for the cold desert night and were kept awake shivering under a bright white moon. A week later, fully prepared with new Arizona sweatshirts and wool socks, we were kept up by an intense heat that didn't drop below 100 degrees until two o'clock in the morning. I wasn't bothered much by the lack of sleep because I was deeply fascinated with the Saguaro cacti surrounding us. They can live for nearly 200 years, and when you're near you can feel an otherworldly wisdom about them. These majestic cacti are stitched beneath their warm, cantaloupe sun.

Materials

Pattern template (found on page 140)

Pen, pencil or water-soluble marker

100% cotton fabric

6-inch (15-cm) embroidery hoop

Size 5 needle

6-strand embroidery floss
(see DMC® Color Guide below)

Fabric scissors and sewing snips

Stitch List

Satin stitch (page 14)

French knot (page 11)

Seed stitch (page 15)

3824 Warm Cantaloupe

3827 Peaches and Cream

580 Avocado Green

3826 Terracotta

3863 Cobblestone Beige

739 Ivory

437 Desert Sand

989 Spring Green

986 Cactus Green

435 Golden Brown

369 Light Matcha

898 Pecan

Warm Desert Mirage
(continued)

1. Start by tracing the pattern template with your pen, pencil or water-soluble marker onto the fabric using the Preparing Your Hoop guide (page 19).

2. Begin using satin stitches to fill in the setting sun. Use 2 strands of floss (page 21) for this step. Stitch the sun using warm cantaloupe (3824).

3. When you're finished with the sun, you can begin stitching the cliffside with 2 strands of floss. Use French knots for this step. For the smaller areas, use terracotta (3826). Fill in the rest of the space with peaches and cream (3827).

4. Next, use 3 strands of cobblestone beige (3863) to make the next layer of earth with seed stitches. Now, fill in the leftover spots with pecan (898).

5. Using French knots, start making the next dune. Here, I used 2 strands of floss. Fill this area in with pecan (898). You can always swap French knots for seed stitches if you choose.

6. On the dune directly to the right of the last one, fill in the area with seed stitches. Fill most of the area with pecan (898), but make sure to leave some space for another texture element. I used 3 strands of floss here.

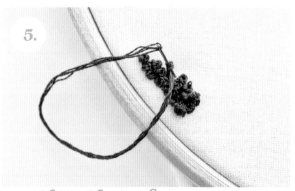

7. The second to last layer will be stitched with seed stitches. I alternated between pecan (898), desert sand (437) and golden brown (435) for this step.

8. For the last layer, use 2 strands of floss to fill in the area with French knots. I alternated evenly between desert sand (437) and golden brown (435).

9. For the rest of the pattern, we'll be using satin stitches to create the yucca and saguaro cacti. I used 3 strands of floss for this. Use light matcha green (369) for the yucca. The closest saguaro uses cactus green (986), the tallest uses avocado green (580) and the shortest uses spring green (989).

10. Now you're ready to stitch the spikes on the cacti. I used 1 strand of ivory (739) for this. Make the spikes using tiny seed stitches. Push your needle up through the back of the fabric into the middle of the cactus satin stitches and then back down a very slight distance away from your entry point. Repeat sporadically on each saguaro cacti.

11. Finally, you're finished with your project and can now close your hoop off using your desired technique (page 22).

Blooming Prickly Pear Cactus

As deep as my love runs for the saguaro cacti, no desert bloom grips my admiration and nostalgia like the prickly pear cacti. Brilliantly creating a network of green prickly paddles, they stretch out and crown themselves with vibrant flowers and buds. Prickly pears were some of my very first embroideries to make because, living in West Texas at the time, I was always surrounded by them. We used to ride around the ranch we grew up on in the back of my granddad's truck. I'm not sure what it was about them, but my dad and granddad loved taking out their pocket knives and cutting into the cactus paddles to say, "Look how much water is inside here!" Maybe because water is a hot commodity in those parts, or maybe because they were infatuated with desert life, either way their love for desert creatures was passed on to me, and I'm excited to share that love with you in the form of a fiber-art cactus.

Materials

Pattern template (found on page 145)

Pen, pencil or water-soluble marker

100% cotton fabric

6-inch (15-cm) embroidery hoop

Size 5 needle

6-strand embroidery floss
(see DMC® Color Guide below)

Fabric scissors and sewing snips

Stitch List

Satin stitch (page 14)

Seed stitch (page 15)

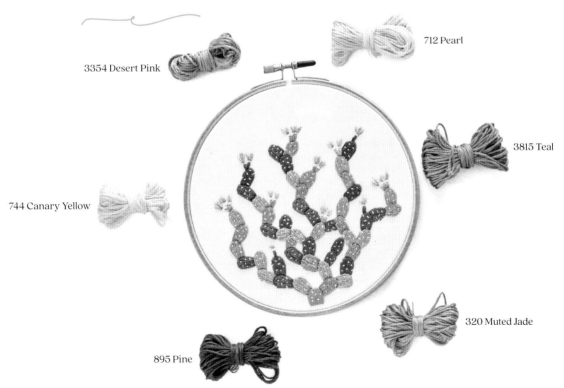

3354 Desert Pink

712 Pearl

3815 Teal

744 Canary Yellow

320 Muted Jade

895 Pine

1. Start by tracing the pattern template with your pen, pencil or water-soluble marker onto the fabric using the Preparing Your Hoop guide (page 19).

2. Begin using satin stitches to fill in the paddles of the cactus plant. Use 3 strands of floss (page 21) for this step. I alternated between teal (3815), muted jade (320) and pine (895) to add color dimension and movement to the piece. Use the same holes from the top of the previous paddle to keep your stitches as close together as possible.

3. When you're finished with the body of the cactus, use seed stitches to add the pearl (712) prickles. Use 1 strand of floss for this step. Push your needle up through the back of the fabric into the middle of the cactus paddle satin stitches and then back down a very slight distance away from your entry point. Repeat on each paddle.

4. Using satin stitches and the same colors of the paddles, create a mini lump on top of the flowered cactus paddles. Use 3 strands of floss for this step.

(continued)

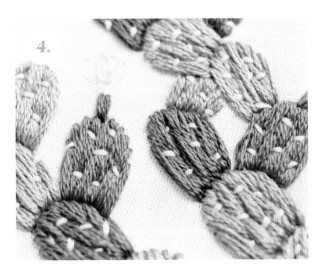

Blooming Prickly Pear Cactus (*continued*)

5. Next, use 2 strands of canary yellow (744) to make the base of each flower. Use satin stitches for this step.

6. Now use desert pink (3354) to make the flower blooms. Don't worry about perfection on these flowers as they're meant to have a little character with a jagged edge. Use satin stitches for this step.

7. Finally, you're finished with your project and can now close your hoop off using your desired technique (page 22).

5.

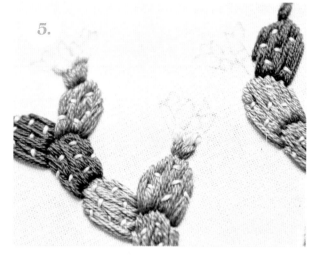

6.

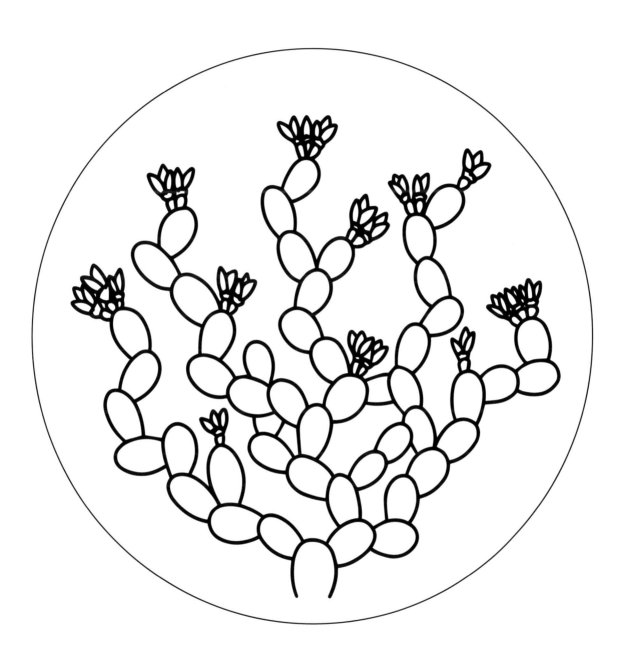

Dewy Opalescent Succulents

This *Echeveria elegans* is one of the most popular succulents, and for good reason. Succulents look like blue-green flowers sent straight from outer space. Unfortunately for me, I find succulents the hardest plants to keep alive. Thank goodness for embroidery because this one doesn't need water or sunlight or magic from a galaxy far, far away to stay green. Remember that succulents are quirky souls, and their leaves are intricately and freely placed. You don't have to worry about keeping them straight or perfectly in line with each other while you're tracing your pattern or while you're stitching it. By the end, you'll have a delightful succulent that is purely your own.

Materials

Pattern template (found on page 150)

Pen, pencil or water-soluble marker

100% cotton fabric

6-inch (15-cm) embroidery hoop

Size 5 needle

6-strand embroidery floss
(see DMC® Color Guide below)

Fabric scissors and sewing snips

Stitch List

Satin stitch (page 14)

Long and short stitch (page 13)

Back stitch (page 10)

14 Key Lime

3740 Purple Dusk

564 Pastel Jade

367 Soft Emerald

3836 Desert Purple

3753 Glacier Blue

890 Sacramento Green

712 Pearl

Dewy Opalescent Succulents
(continued)

1. Start by tracing the pattern template with your pen, pencil or water-soluble marker onto the fabric using the Preparing Your Hoop guide (page 19).

2. Begin using satin stitches to fill in the plump leaves at the center of the plant. Use 3 strands of floss (page 21) for this step. Start in the very center of the plant using soft emerald (367), then move outward to the next two rings using key lime (14) and pastel jade (564).

3. When you're finished with the center trio of colors, move on to the next ring. Grab glacier blue (3753) and, with 3 strands of floss, use satin stitches to almost reach the tip of each petal. Fill in the tips of each of these petals using desert purple (3836) and long and short stitches.

4. Continue this method on the final ring of leaves, but this time use key lime (14) again. Use satin stitches almost to the tip of the leaf. Next, using long and short stitches, add soft emerald (367) and desert purple (3836) to the very tip.

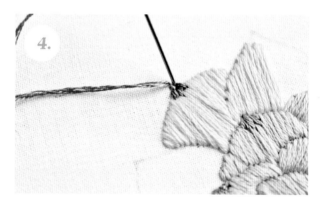

5. Again using satin stitches, you can fill in the spiky cactus leaves. For the spiky leaves, use 3 strands of Sacramento green (890).

6. Using 1 strand of thread, make the little stripes on the spiky cactus with pearl (712). Use back stitches for this step.

7. For the plump, rounded leaves, continue using satin stitches. For the bigger bulbs, use desert purple (3836), and for the smaller bulbs, use pastel jade (564). Use 3 strands of floss for this step.

8. Now stitch the remaining foliage using soft emerald (367). Use 3 strands of floss and satin stitches for this step.

9. Using purple dusk (3740), you can back stitch the stems of the desert purple leaves and soft emerald (367) for the pastel jade leaves in step 7 with 1 strand of floss. Continue using this method for the rest of your stems. Use Sacramento green (890) for the stems of the foliage in step 8.

10. Finally, you're finished with your project and can now close your hoop off using your desired technique (page 22).

Sunrise Over Organ Pipe Cactus

One of the things I love most in nature is when there's a seamless pairing of warm and cool colors, and one of my favorite places I see it is in the desert. If you've ever woken up in a tent in the desert to see the sun rising, I'm sure you've noticed the wild shift in cool blue and purple shadows to warm peachy colors, deep oranges and yellows. This organ pipe cactus takes me right to that brief moment at dawn with both the cool and sunny glow. Because the sun is just rising in this pattern, notice the yellows are barely touching the tallest organ pipes on the cactus. Be free with your stitches to mimic the uneven texture of the cactus as the sun starts to melt over it.

Materials

Pattern template (found on page 155)

Pen, pencil or water-soluble marker

100% cotton fabric

6-inch (15-cm) embroidery hoop

Size 5 needle

6-strand embroidery floss
(see DMC® Color Guide below)

Fabric scissors and sewing snips

Stitch List

Satin stitch (page 14)

Split stitch (page 16)

Seed stitch (page 15)

French knot (page 11)

Back stitch (page 10)

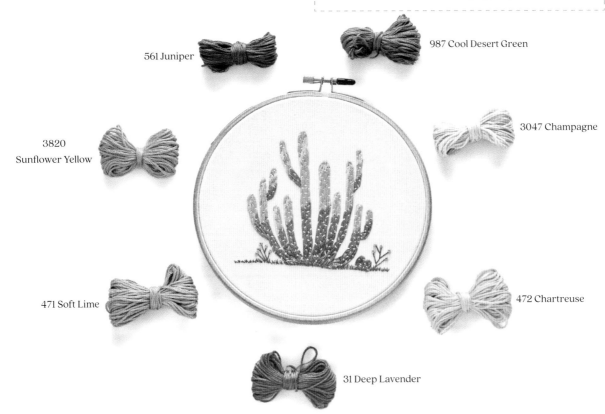

561 Juniper

987 Cool Desert Green

3820 Sunflower Yellow

3047 Champagne

471 Soft Lime

472 Chartreuse

31 Deep Lavender

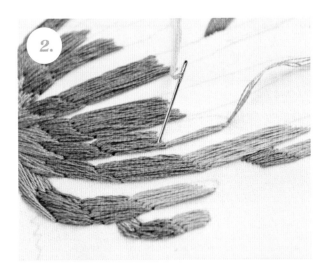

Sunrise Over Organ Pipe Cactus (*continued*)

1. Start by tracing the pattern template with your pen, pencil or water-soluble marker onto the fabric using the Preparing Your Hoop guide (page 19).

2. Begin using satin stitches at the base of the cactus with deep lavender (31). Use 2 strands of floss (page 21) for this step. Stitch your way up the cactus using split stitches, and as you go up, move to juniper (561), cool desert green (987), soft lime (471), chartreuse (472) and, lastly, sunflower yellow (3820). Stairstep the warmer colors as pictured, as if the light is coming from the left.

3. We'll now be using seed stitches to create the prickles of the cactus. I used 1 strand of floss for this. Using champagne (3047), begin creating little seed stitches over your split stitches over the whole piece.

4. Continue using seed stitches to make the mini grass. Use juniper (561) and deep lavender (31) interchangeably. Use 1 strand of floss for this step.

(continued)

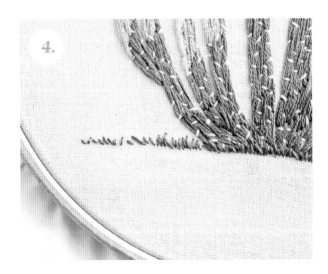

Sunrise Over Organ Pipe Cactus (*continued*)

5. Now, with juniper (561), make the stems of the flowerets using back stitches. Continue using 1 strand of floss.

6. Grab sunflower yellow (3820) again and, using French knots, make the buds of your flowerets. Use 2 strands of floss for this step.

7. Finally, you're finished with your project and can now close your hoop off using your desired technique (page 22).

Wandering Air Plant

Weird and wonderful, my sister is a lover of misplaced things and misplaced people. She finds beauty in things anyone else would easily overlook. We joke that she's a witch. I've watched her care for people in a delicate and peculiar way only she knows how to, and she does it freely and unbothered and it doesn't matter where. She's kind of like an air plant— one of the most bizarre plants ever, found right in the desert. Air plants don't have normal root systems; they're desert wanderers. This wild, desert octopus-like creature normally clings to trees for its life force. It doesn't need soil, so you could keep one just sitting on a sunny shelf in your house if you wanted to. Mainly comprised of long and short stitches, you can be as messy as you want while stitching its arms as you blend the colors together.

Materials

Pattern template (found on page 159)

Pen, pencil or water-soluble marker

100% cotton fabric

6-inch (15.25-cm) embroidery hoop

Size 5 needle

6-strand embroidery floss
(see DMC® Color Guide below)

Fabric scissors and sewing snips

Stitch List

Long and short stitch (page 13)

Back stitch (page 10)

524 Sage Haze Green

3364 Desert Sage

310 Black

778 Dusty Rose

Wandering Air Plant
(continued)

1. Start by tracing the pattern template with your pen, pencil or water-soluble marker onto the fabric using the Preparing Your Hoop guide (page 19).

2. Begin using long and short stitches to fill in the tentacles of the air plant. Use 2 strands of floss (page 21) for this step. You'll use sage haze green (524) for the center of the plant, desert sage (3364) for the middle of each arm and dusty rose (778) for the edges. I used long and short stitches so the colors would easily blend together with minimal effort and because I could easily create curves. Simply stick your needle directly into the previous stitches.

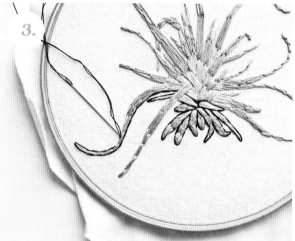

3. When you're finished with the tentacles of the plant, grab black (310) and, using 1 strand of floss, begin following along the edges of the plant to better accentuate each arm. Use back stitches for this step.

4. Finally, you're finished with your project and can now close your hoop off using your desired technique (page 22).

urban jungle

House plants are king in modern embroidery (and many other art forms) in recent years. They're essential in our house, as I want to be surrounded by them. Not only is our house decorated in its own jungle, it's decorated in embroidered plants too. If you're working your way through this book from top to bottom, by now your house is decorated with plant embroideries too! If I'm ever feeling down, the plant store is my go-to place. There's nothing like walking down the green aisles of plants looking for the ones that stick out to you, picking out new pots and spending the rest of the day freeing their roots and refreshing their soil. Indoor plants become deeply personal somehow, and you have to take extra good care of them because they know all of your secrets. As you wander through this chapter, you'll stitch the indoor plants that have captured my soul and the ones I don't think I'll ever be able to live without!

Monstrous Majestic Monstera

I think the monstera is the most curious potted plant. It's the most curious plant in the wild, too. Their leaves have slits and holes to prevent tearing in deep-soaking rainfall in the rain forest, so it makes it kind of funny to see them indoors. I just love the jungle feeling they add to interiors, but I've had a hard time keeping them alive longer than a few months. Thankfully, embroideries don't need to be watered! I'm introducing the weave stitch (page 17) in this pattern, which is a deceivingly easy stitch. It looks intricate and complicated, but it's simply a back stitch and a little up and over needle weaving. You can also give this plant basket some texture with French knots (page 11), or you can use satin stitches (page 14) and any color pattern you want!

Materials

Pattern template (found on page 166)

Pen, pencil or water-soluble marker

100% cotton fabric

6-inch (15-cm) embroidery hoop

Size 5 needle

6-strand embroidery floss
(see DMC® Color Guide below)

Fabric scissors and sewing snips

Stitch List

Weave stitch (page 17)

Back stitch (page 10)

Satin stitch (page 14)

310 Black

500 Midnight Emerald

986 Cactus Green

469 Moss Green

898 Pecan

3862 Soft Walnut

738 Cream

Monstrous Majestic Monstera (*continued*)

1. Start by tracing the pattern template with your pen, pencil or water-soluble marker onto the fabric using the Preparing Your Hoop guide (page 19).

2. With 2 strands (page 21) of floss and using cream (738) and soft walnut (3862), you can begin making the basket with weave stitches.

3. When you're finished with the basket, take pecan (898) with 3 strands of floss and, using back stitches, make your plant stand.

4. Begin using satin stitches to create your monstera leaves using moss green (469), cactus green (986) and midnight emerald (500). Start from one side of each leaf and push your needle into the center of the leaf. Continue this until you've covered one whole side of the leaf. Repeat this on the other side, but this time push your needle into the same holes you already created down the center of the leaves. Use 2 strands of floss for this step. Repeat for each leaf.

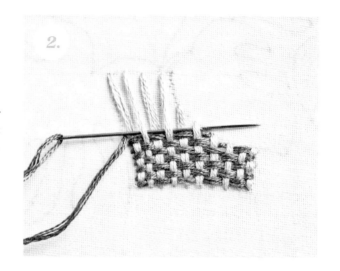

5. When you're finished with your satin stitches, use 1 strand of thread and back stitches to add a stem to the middle of the leaves, matching each leaf's respective color. Continue with this step using 2 strands of thread to add the rest of your stems leading to the basket. Repeat for each leaf.

6. Next, use 1 strand of black (310) to outline everything using back stitches. This will leave crisp edges to the leaves and better outline each element of the piece.

7. From the center of each leaf, add your color dimension. Push your needle up through the back of the fabric into the middle of the leaf satin stitches and then back down along the edges of the leaf. Repeat on each leaf. For the midnight emerald leaf, use cactus green (986). For the moss green leaves, use cactus green (986). For the cactus green leaves, use midnight emerald (500). Use 1 strand of floss for this step.

8. Finally, you're finished with your project and can now close your hoop off using your desired technique (page 22).

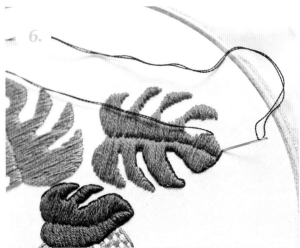

Dreamy Verdant Hanging Plants

My favorite indoor plants in embroidery (and in real life) are earthward, cascading, deep green, hanging plants. There's at least one ivy in every room of our house, so of course I had to include a pattern dedicated to them. This arrangement has some smaller details, so I worked with a thinner thread thickness. I chose a pastel color palette for the pots to give it an even more lively spring feeling. It may look complicated, but the colors in this pattern are reused throughout and it's mainly comprised of satin stitches. If you're like me, you'll want to nestle in your coziest pajamas with this pattern and rewatch *You've Got Mail*, the best spring-embroidery-stitch-session companion out there.

Materials

Pattern template (found on page 171)

Pen, pencil or water-soluble marker

100% cotton fabric

6-inch (15-cm) embroidery hoop

Size 5 needle

6-strand embroidery floss
(see DMC® Color Guide below)

Fabric scissors and sewing snips

Stitch List

Satin stitch (page 14)

Back stitch (page 10)

French knot (page 11)

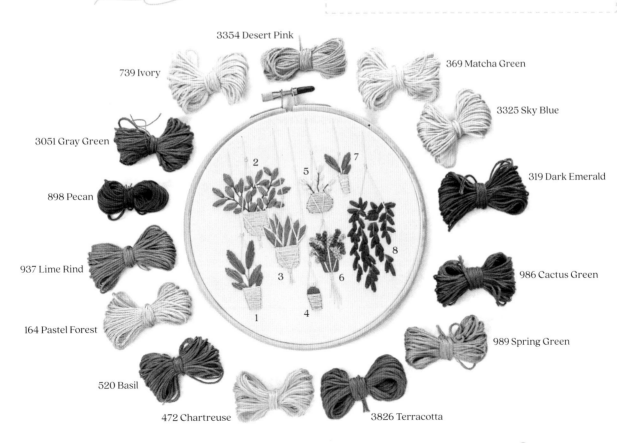

3354 Desert Pink

739 Ivory

369 Matcha Green

3325 Sky Blue

3051 Gray Green

319 Dark Emerald

898 Pecan

937 Lime Rind

986 Cactus Green

164 Pastel Forest

989 Spring Green

520 Basil

472 Chartreuse

3826 Terracotta

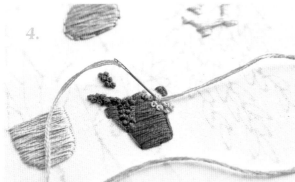

1. Start by tracing the pattern template with your pen, pencil or water-soluble marker onto the fabric using the Preparing Your Hoop guide (page 19).

2. Begin using satin stitches to fill in the plant pots. Use 2 strands of floss (page 21) for this step. I changed between pastel forest (164), desert pink (3354), sky blue (3325) and terracotta (3826) for each planter. Make sure when stitching the pots with the plants that drape over the side to leave space for the foliage that we'll add later.

3. Outline your pots using 1 strand of floss. Use back stitches for this step. Outline each planter using its coordinating color from the previous step.

4. When you're finished with the planters, you can begin stitching the plants. For the bushy plant in the terracotta pot, I changed between spring green (989) and cactus green (986). Use French knots for this step. Remember, you can easily switch out French knots with seed stitches (page 15) if you prefer.

5. For ease of reading, I have numbered the plants from 1 through 8, read from left to right. When stitching plants 1, 2, 7 and 8, use the same method of satin stitches. Use 3 strands of floss for this step. For plants 1 and 7, use gray green (3051). For plant 2, I alternated between basil (520) and lime rind (937). For plant 8, use dark emerald (319). I like to start stitching from the middle of the leaf and work my way down each side to create the shape. Notice how you can use the hole at the base of the leaf multiple times here too.

(continued)

Dreamy Verdant Hanging Plants *(continued)*

6. Next, use 2 strands of lime rind (937) to make the long body of plant 3 with satin stitches. Don't worry about perfection because you'll outline this plant with chartreuse (472). To outline, use 2 strands and back stitches.

7. With 2 strands of floss and satin stitches, use the same rounded shape for both plants 4 and 5. Plant 4 uses basil (520) for the cactus and chartreuse (472) for the flower on top. For plant 5, use matcha green (369).

8. For the rest of the pattern, we'll be using back stitches to create the stems of the plants and the jute rope. I used 1 strand of floss for this. Use pecan (898) for the branches of plant 2 and lime rind (937) for the stems of plants 1, 5, 7 and 8.

9. Now you're ready to stitch the jute rope for the hanging plants. Use 1 strand of ivory (739) for this. Notice how between some of the back stitches there are little bits of satin stitches to create a knot effect.

10. Finally, you're finished with your project and can now close your hoop off using your desired technique (page 22).

Flourishing Propagation Station

Plant propagation is what first made me fall in love with indoor plants. I was at an estate sale and found an assortment of jars with different plant cuttings inside them. I quickly became obsessed with growing full plants from a single leaf in water. I later learned that my Great-Grandma Mickey used to keep plant cuttings all along her windows and that gave me another reason to love and cultivate my own urban jungle. This trio of plants is a pilea, which almost looks like a mini lily pad plant, a fishbone cactus and a parlor palm. You could also try adding some of the ivies from the Dreamy Verdant Hanging Plants pattern (page 167) for your own verdant propagation station.

Materials

Pattern template (found on page 175)

Pen, pencil or water-soluble marker

100% cotton fabric

6-inch (15-cm) embroidery hoop

Size 5 needle

6-strand embroidery floss
(see DMC® Color Guide below)

Fabric scissors and sewing snips

Stitch List

Back stitch (page 10)

Satin stitch (page 14)

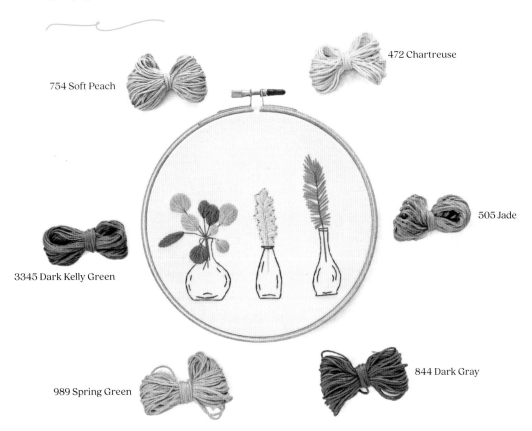

754 Soft Peach

472 Chartreuse

505 Jade

3345 Dark Kelly Green

989 Spring Green

844 Dark Gray

Flourishing Propagation Station (*continued*)

1. Start by tracing the pattern template with your pen, pencil or water-soluble marker onto the fabric using the Preparing Your Hoop guide (page 19).

2. Begin using medium-length back stitches to fill in the blades of the palm cutting. Use 2 strands of floss (page 21) for this step and jade (505). Use 1 strand of dark Kelly green (3345) to create the stem.

3. For the middle plant, use satin stitches along one side of the leaf using 3 strands of chartreuse (472). Continue on the other side using the holes created down the middle of the leaf. Now you can outline the curly leaf and make the stem with soft peach (754) back stitches. Use 2 strands for the outside of the leaf and 1 strand for the stem.

4. Next, use 2 strands of floss to make the circular leaves of the pilea plant with satin stitches. To create a rounded shape for the leaves, you can keep bringing the needle down into the fabric at the base of the bud using the same hole multiple times. I alternated between spring green (989) and dark Kelly green (3345) for this step. Use 1 strand of dark Kelly green (3345) to create the stems with back stitches.

5. For the rest of the pattern, we'll be using back stitches to create the jars and vases. I used 1 strand of floss for this. Back stitches don't have to be the same length, although they generally are. I used dark gray (844) for this step.

6. Finally, you're finished with your project and can now close your hoop off using your desired technique (page 22).

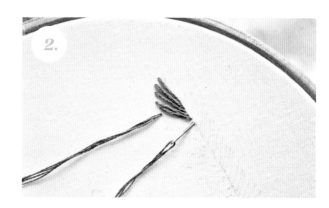

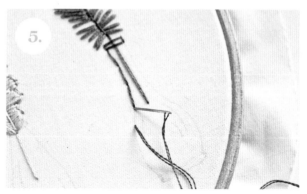

Poised Prayer Plant

Prayer plants are some of the most unique and memorable house plants. They're called prayer plants because during the day they lie flat soaking in the sun and at night they close up like praying hands. I'm thoroughly enchanted by hot pink in plants, and I adore the contrast with shades of green. I chose to use a soft ruby color for my fabric to emphasize their complementary colors. Stitching this pattern is particularly satisfying to work on because you're mainly using one stitch and changing shades of green. You don't have to worry about perfection with long and short stitches because the edges should be uneven to better blend the greens of the leaf. Enjoy working with this meditative plant and maybe challenge yourself with new fabric colors.

Materials

Pattern template (found on page 180)

Pen, pencil or water-soluble marker

100% cotton fabric

6-inch (15-cm) embroidery hoop

Size 5 needle

6-strand embroidery floss
(see DMC® Color Guide below)

Fabric scissors and sewing snips

Stitch List

Satin stitch (page 14)

Long and short stitch (page 13)

Back stitch (page 10)

369 Matcha Green

3826 Terracotta

703
Summer Green

150 Cranberry

890 Sacramento Green

Poised Prayer Plant
(continued)

1. Start by tracing the pattern template with your pen, pencil or water-soluble marker onto the fabric using the Preparing Your Hoop guide (page 19).

2. Begin with the cranberry (150) leaves using 2 strands of floss (page 21). Use satin stitches for this step.

3. Now using long and short stitches, you can fill in first layer of each leaf. Use 2 strands of floss and summer green (703) for this step.

4. Using long and short stitches, grab Sacramento green (890) for the next layer. Here, you will continue using 2 strands of floss.

5. For the final and middle layer, use long and short stitches again. Like the other layers, this layer still has two sides. Stitch along one side, then continue on the second side using the same holes you've already created down the center of the leaf. Use light matcha green (369) for this step.

6. When you're finished with the green body for the leaf, take cranberry (150) and, using 1 strand of floss, begin adding in the stems. Push your needle up through the back of the fabric into the middle of the leaf long and short stitches and then back down into the base of the flower using back stitches. Continue using this method for the stem down the middle.

7. Outline your leaves with Sacramento green (890) back stitches. Use 2 strands of floss for this step.

8. Using back stitches, you can now make your stems. Use 2 strands of Sacramento green (890) for this step.

9. Now you're ready to stitch your pot using terracotta (3826). Use 3 strands of floss and satin stitches here. I slanted each row of satin stitches in opposite directions, to give my piece more texture and visual interest.

10. You can now outline your pot with back stitches using 1 strand of floss. Continue using terracotta (3826) for this step.

11. Finally, you're finished with your project and can now close your hoop off using your desired technique (page 22).

Fiddle-Leaf Fig Foliage

I'm concluding this book with an homage to one of my dearest house plants. They're just the best. You get to have a mini tree in your house! They're very finicky though, and it's been rumored that they like it when you sway them around, simulating wind. Apparently it helps them grow stronger. After reading this, I got my morning coffee, settled in next to her and gently started shaking her. My husband walked out and said, "It's a windy one today!" He gets me. As always, if you have the "magic" touch that turns your houseplants yellow, this project is your hassle-free solution. The best part of fiddle-leaf figs is the network of strong veins running through their leaves. I wanted to highlight that in this pattern, so if you want to work on your back stitch you've come to the right place!

Materials

Pattern template (found on page 184)

Pen, pencil or water-soluble marker

100% cotton fabric

6-inch (15-cm) embroidery hoop

Size 5 needle

6-strand embroidery floss
(see DMC® Color Guide below)

Fabric scissors and sewing snips

Stitch List

Back stitch (page 10)

Split stitch (page 16)

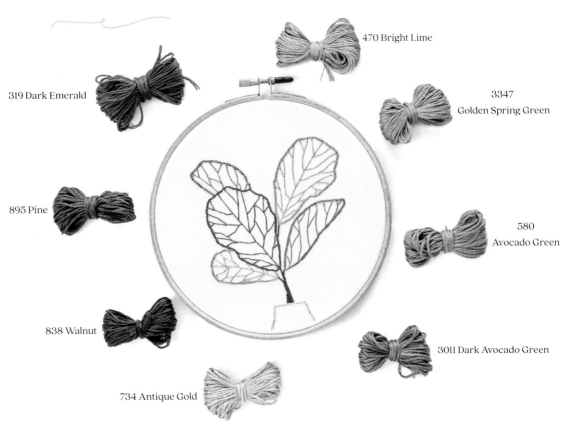

470 Bright Lime

319 Dark Emerald

3347 Golden Spring Green

895 Pine

580 Avocado Green

838 Walnut

3011 Dark Avocado Green

734 Antique Gold

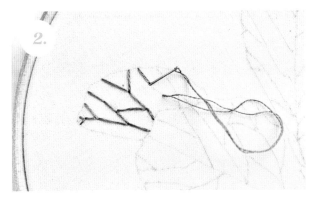

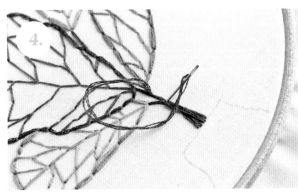

Fiddle-Leaf Fig Foliage
(continued)

1. Start by tracing the pattern template with your pen, pencil or water-soluble marker onto the fabric using the Preparing Your Hoop guide (page 19).

2. Begin using back stitches to stitch the veins and stems of your leaves. Use 2 strands (page 21) of floss for the veins and 3 strands for the stems. There are three variations of these leaves: dark green, where the outside is dark emerald (319) and the middle is pine (895); lime, where the outside is golden spring green (3347) and the middle is bright lime (470); and olive, where the outside is dark avocado green (3011) and the middle is avocado green (580).

3. When you're finished with the stems and veins of the body of each leaf, continue using back stitches to follow along the outer edges of the leaves. Use 3 strands of floss for this step.

4. Next, use 2 strands of walnut (838) to make the branch with split stitches. Use back stitches for the thinner areas at the base of each leaf.

5. Again using 2 strands of thread and back stitches, take antique gold (734) and follow along the edge of the vase.

6. Finally, you're finished with your project and can now close your hoop off using your desired technique (page 22).

acknowledgments

This creative journey has been an immeasurable blessing to me, and I couldn't have done it without my people. I'm deeply thankful to everyone who's supported me in what I do and those who have liked, shared, purchased and stitched with me.

A proper and deep thank you to my husband, Christian. Thank you for supporting me so unwaveringly, for showing me the universe with childlike wonder and for handing me cups of coffee and pulling me out of the house for walks to clear my head when I'm creatively stuck. You make amazing tacos and I like you.

Thank you to my dad for teaching me to love plants and appreciate the little things.

Thank you to my mom for teaching me I am enough, and that I can create and do whatever I want.

Thank you to Nana and Papa for teaching me to try new and grand things any chance I get.

Thank you to Mimi and Granddad for teaching me to garden and to care for wild creatures.

Thank you to my siblings, John, Luke, Sophie, Sam and Charlie, for teaching me friendship and making me laugh no matter what life is up to. And thanks to Anne for just as much friendship and laughter and for helping me wind thread.

Thank you to the Schnückers for your eternal kindness, warmth and support.

Thank you to my family and friends for always reinspiring me.

Thank you to my embroidery community and followers. Your support and messages and purchases are no small thing to me. From the bottom of my heart, thank you. This book is for you.

And an extra-special thank you to Page Street Publishing for reaching out to me about this grand project, helping make my book-writing dreams a reality and for giving me so much creative freedom. Also, special thanks to Emily, Sarah, Rosie and Meg for your patience and for believing in my work.

Maggie Schnücker is an embroidery artist currently living in the greater Houston area of Texas with her husband, Christian; her dog, Georgia; and her cat, Trout. Maggie studied graphic design at Abilene Christian University and has been a longtime lover of the arts. She began sharing her work on Instagram as @maggiejosstudio in 2017, and she has since cultivated a following of more than 91,000 there. Since then, she has sold thousands of patterns and taught many creatives her favorite craft.

Maggie is also a digital artist and painter and has had her works picked up by major retailers, including HomeGoods®. She has been featured in *Love Embroidery*, *Voyage Houston* and more. To find more about Maggie and to shop finished embroidery pieces, visit maggiejosstudio.com and join her monthly subscription, Flourish, for even more embroidery patterns.

index